SHIFTING/OPTICS

SHIFTING OPTICS

A Life/*in Perspective*

DUNG DUONG

COPYRIGHT © 2020 DUNG DUONG
All rights reserved.

SHIFTING OPTICS
A Life, in Perspective

ISBN   978-1-5445-1534-2 *Hardcover*
          978-1-5445-1533-5 *Paperback*
          978-1-5445-1532-8 *Ebook*

To my kids:

When I started this book, your biggest complaint was having to read an hour a day and write a short summary. I hope that when you read this book, that is still your biggest problem. Unfortunately, life is more difficult and much harsher.

I wish I could prepare you for everything that you will encounter as you grow, but I know that I am neither that knowledgeable nor that good of a prognosticator. You will face failures, ostracization, heartbreaks, and times when you do not know how to move forward.

What I went through will be different and not germane to what you are facing. Still, I hope you find perspective from this book. I hope you find solace and comfort in knowing that however unique are your problems, you are not alone in having them. I hope you recognize how important you are to making your world better. I hope you find your way through.

Daddy loves you.

* * *

To you, the reader:

I started this book-writing journey hoping to offer a story that would allow you to gain perspective on your own life—the kind of perspective that counts when you need it most. These are tales of perseverance through the worst of times, of being able to steadfastly keep my eyes open even when every essence of me wanted them shut. I have grown from this experience, having a much deeper understanding of myself—and also a greater appreciation for my immediate, close, and distant family.

I dedicate this book to them—and to you. And to anyone who wants to make the world better, willing to use that as their guiding light. Here, I hope you find fun, find that smile, and most importantly, find your way through.

CONTENTS

INTRODUCTION 9

1. PURPOSE LIGHTING THE WAY 15

2. ON A MISSION 41

3. DARKER DAYS 63

4. COMING OF AGE 77

5. SURVIVAL 105

6. WE END AT THE BEGINNING 119

   CONCLUSION 129

   ACKNOWLEDGMENTS 133

   ABOUT THE AUTHOR 139

INTRODUCTION

Postwar Vietnam was not the best place to raise a child. Especially a child who had been laying for days in the NICU, eyes still shut.

I was delivered via Cesarean by a French doctor, a doctor my mom specifically wanted to deliver me—so specifically, in fact, that it all went down a day before he was forced to leave the country.

I was relatively healthy for being a couple months early (it's hard for me to remember the exact timing of it all). I didn't have hair or fingernails, that sort of thing. But from all indications, I was relatively healthy.

The problem was one of optics: I just didn't open my eyes. There was serious talk of terminating me after birth. It was hard enough for my parents to raise a normally-abled child in that environment—one where soldiers had occupied their home, the family property was ransacked, society was in a state of turmoil—you name it. How hard would my life have been, having been blind without access to the necessary resources? How hard would their lives have been? What would that sacrifice have looked like?

Luckily, those decisions did not need to be made. On Day Three, I opened my eyes.

* * *

Hey, you, holding this book...I see you.

My eyes opened, remember?

I know the world feels hard sometimes. Maybe you've had moments where you've felt lost, moments where you, as an adult, haven't been able to open your own eyes or heart in the face of the challenges ahead of and around you. Situations can feel heavy and disheartening. Situations where you feel that the hole is so deep that daylight seems faint. I know this, trust me.

Something struck me when working on this book: my daughter had an accident on the playground, and one of the questions the nurse asked her at the hospital—which, the nurse assured me, she asks every child these days—is whether or not my daughter ever had thought of harming herself.

She asked this *of a child*.

Here, in the United States of America, we've gotten to a point where the nurses have to ask these questions—and where, presumably, some kids say yes to them.

That is heartbreaking to me.

I have lived a full life, which I will share with you in this book: I've fled a third-world country by boat, lived in refugee camps, been homeless and jailed, immigrated to the United States, grown up in poverty, came of age in the Western world, got an education, started a family of my own, developed businesses, and invested in companies that mean something. Some of these things have been more challenging than others, but they've all played a part—whether large or small—in making me who I am today.

Who I am today, by the way, is a short Asian guy who wears shorts year-round. Who focuses on leaving the world better than he found it. Who could bore you to death (but won't, or will try not to) about the ins and outs of the fundamentals of optics and engineering. Who, despite being pretty smart, once voluntarily climbed into the middle of a kickboxing ring—after paying fifty dollars for a ticket (which was never refunded)—in something called a "Bone Brawl." Oh, and while *on a date*. A guy whose name—Dung (pronounced "Young")—has been the butt of many Westerners' jokes, like "A Boy Named Sue." Who has always, sort of, had to fight through things just a little bit more.

We'll get to all that later—all that, and then some.

Here's the point: I have faced hardships, and I will share those with you. I have been low, low to the point where I have stared into the eyes of mortality. I'm writing this book to offer my stories, my honest recollections, so that you—and, truthfully, my children who will someday read this—can take from them *perspective*. To open *your* eyes to the fact that there's always a way through.

I hope you—and they—can find a nugget or two in this book that shows the value in being intrinsically motivated to *do* better, to *be* better as a person and member of society. That shows that if you have the talent in something, you have a responsibility to use it to help the world. That shows you can persevere, even through the hardest of hard times. Stay true to yourself. Remain rational through turmoil. Act with integrity. Keep a strong mind and a strong will. Life can be as complicated as you make it, so simplify as much as possible. Keep everything in perspective.

If you—and my kids—get nothing like that here, I hope you at least get a snicker at one or two of my jokes every now and then.

Let's take it from the top. And by the top, I mean present day.

chapter / one

PURPOSE LIGHTING THE WAY

Vietnam, 1979. We are taking a small boat to a larger boat out at sea. It's supposed to be a quick trip to Thailand. We are covered by a burlap tarp to avoid being seen. When I look through the holes, I see soldiers walking by. My mom has a death grip over my mouth to keep me quiet.

* * *

This is called *Shifting Optics* for a reason. Optics is not only a way to describe our perception of circumstances or problems but it is also the technical field in which I've tried to lend my knowledge and make my mark.

Most recently, I did that through my work at Fluence Bioengineering, where we produced technology to facilitate vertical farming and other sustainable horticultural processes. This is critical because, as many report, we will need a 70 percent increase in the amount of crops we grow by 2050 to meet the rise in population. While I believe this date is pessimistic, this does not alleviate the need for technological innovation to secure a primary need for mankind. Even today when the world grows more food than necessary, millions die of hunger each year and more than half the population deals with a lack of food on a regular basis. What happens when population growth coupled with declining food production due to climate change further reduces the excess in crop production? How many more will die of hunger?

In 2018, my partners and I sold a horticulture lighting company to a much larger entity with global reach. My motivation was that they could spread our technology faster. I wanted to push into the global markets and make growing produce more efficient and cost-effective. The goal was to innovate and develop technology in industries with high-value crops (medicinal) so that the technology, most importantly the cost of that technology, could be applied to low-value crops. While the current buzz is vertical farming, this method of growing will only supplement the food supply (not a panacea to the pending global food shortage). There is much work to be done in controlled environment agriculture to ensure everyone gets fed in the future.

Why have I landed here? Because I know what it's like to go without food. I have been hungry. Then and now, my mission is the same: I want to feed the world.

I am now at a point to help in that mission, and others, by supporting startups and organizations that also aim to help the world.

But it took some time to arrive at this place, at this ability to help.

From building and selling a company, to walking up and down Sand Hill Road to raise tens of millions, to driving out to the middle of nowhere to test a biological agent detection system—and every fork in the road along the way—there have been aspects of my personality that have served me well. The chronology isn't as important as the perspective I took away from each of these experiences and that I hope to share here. I've been able to aggregate information and connect both people and ideas, for example. I'm introverted but can easily start a conversation. When someone says it's impossible to do something, I've always wanted to do it. The fundamentals are all the same across engineering disciplines and corporate functions. Whether it's electrical, mechanical, or optical engineering, it's fairly interesting to notice that the same basic equations apply. Whether it's operations or sales, the fundamental, commonsense lean processes are fairly similar. (I'll go into my work more later.

For now, you just need to know that I've pulled way more all-nighters since college than I did in college.)

So, yes, I've been successful in my life. Now, I have the time and resources to give back and do more for my family and others, here and abroad.

This is true even though my friends would warn you not to go to lunch with me because I am the cheapest guy in the group. (They may have a point. If I grab myself a Starbucks coffee, I don't eat lunch to make up the difference. And yet my wife still thinks I'm fat.)

A large part of my day-to-day now is investing in and supporting companies that make a difference.

First and foremost: more important than any company or any investments is my family. I've been married to my wife since 2007, and we have three kids. I admit that I'm a "tiger dad," but my biggest worry is whether my kids will have the perspective in life to push through. I do tend to be harder on them than most other parents I know. They have a nanny who does everything for them. We live in a gated community. They don't understand the world or how hard it can be. And no, I'm not saying I want them to face hardships in the world, but I do want them to see it. Right now, their biggest struggle in life is me making them read and do math problems that are more advanced than their age.

My hope is that I can teach them to become intrinsically motivated to do better for themselves and our world. That they know they can work through challenging circumstances. That they can see there is light at the other side of a problem and have confidence to rely on themselves to make it to that other side. That there is hope.

Like every parent, I don't have everything figured out, and I don't know quite how to offer them the perspective that will teach them those things. But this book is part of my effort.

My sister, who is three years older than me, is the most influential woman in my life. She always will be, in large part because she practically raised me. But she also played a hand in how I met my wife—because it happened at her first wedding anniversary.

My sister had invited my now-wife there as a potential date for another one of their *other* single friends. She went to the same Buddhist temple as my brother-in-law's mother, and everyone liked her. I was just flying in from Texas to Virginia to visit my sister—an "extra" in the group. On top of that, I'd always expressed that I would never marry a Vietnamese woman because I was too Americanized. I mean, I was the only Asian in my college class in the middle of Indiana, if that tells you anything. So it's no wonder they didn't try to set us up.

I'd arrived on a Friday night. Saturday morning, we were making lunch, and the Vietnamese women were all in the kitchen. Many of the guys didn't jump in, but I like being in the mix. Not that I can cook well, but I can chop things. I can sous-chef.

In this case, it was more like a "woo"-chef.

The group of women were sorting herbs, which are common in most Vietnamese dishes. As they sorted, I joked with them. When lunch was ready, they called everyone to go eat. The beautiful woman who is now my wife didn't get up, so I picked her up and moved her out to the table. I thought I was being smooth, I guess.

But I've never really been smooth, which *may* be why later that day, I ended up with her *and the guy everyone intended to set her up with* in my back seat, while I did donuts in my little sedan. At the time, I was trying to be playful so they would talk to each other more.

Later in the day, more friends showed up, including another young woman who I found very cute. I enjoyed the company of both women and everyone at the gathering, and we had a fun weekend. I exchanged contact information with the women before I returned to Texas, where I emailed them regularly just to say hi and check in. At the time, I thought it all was pretty much for fun.

I did fly up and see my now-wife in Virginia Beach. I didn't think of it as a date, but the story is that she certainly did. We went to Kings Dominion, an amusement park a couple hours away, on our first "date." We got together every month after that, with her coming to see me or vice versa.

One big thing about me is that I am a pleaser, but I don't forgive people easily. It's also true that once I realize I'm wrong, I don't fight anymore. While these personality quirks make me who I am and have served me well throughout my life, it also makes it difficult for long-lasting relationships to develop and persevere. It took a strong, aggressive, smart, and unyielding woman to break through my personality quirks.

CONSCIOUS FUNDING TODAY

Giving back is a huge part of my wife's personality, which she instilled in me. We talk all the time about teaching our kids about perspective through our giving. She started Perspective Charity, which is part scholarship program, part mission-based trips to provide educational supplies. Perspective's vision is to enable children born into any socioeconomic situation the opportunity to become impactful. The purpose is to connect families with kids who are roughly the same age—one in the US and one abroad—so they can all experience what life is like for the other. Each gains another world's perspective; each learns how they can make the world around them better. The nonprofit continues to evolve.

I also invest in a startup that focuses on bridging the education accessibility gap through technology. When the CEO told me of the number of children on the free lunch program and how a lot of those children's only meal of the day comes from free lunches, it reminded me of my own struggles in my youth. Then there's another startup that focuses not only on leadership training and onboarding but on the empathy behind the messaging. This is important because I've seen how good leadership can make up for deficiencies within an organization—and also how bad leadership can turn transformative companies into mediocre ones, dampening their impact. I am also a limited partner in an angel venture capital firm that allows for targeted allocation, where I've invested in organic healing medicines, security, and others. In the past, I've invested in a biotech company aimed at revolutionizing the point-of-care market to improve public health. And today, I also give back by mentoring students from my alma mater, then form strategies to move their business ideas forward.

Long story short? Life is good today, but it took a lot of twists and turns to get here.

LOOKING BACK: MAKING MY WAY TO AUSTIN

Originally, when I came to Austin (my home today), it was supposed to be a three-month internship, not a long-term arrangement. I was a fresh-faced, fresh-out-of-college kid. And yes, my college nickname for a while was also "Fresh." (Coupled with my first name...yeah.)

Prior to moving south, I'd interviewed at three different schools for PhD programs, and all gave me full scholarships with stipends. I chose the Optical Science Center at the University of Arizona, excited at the chance to work under the dean of optics there. I graduated college on a Saturday, drove to Austin on Sunday, and started an internship the next day. It was the summer before my PhD program was to start.

My internship was at an incubator that had received significant venture funding, and I was happy to be on board. I distinctly remember my interview process: a long day of interviews with practically everyone at the company at the time (CEO, fellow engineers, and founders). At our wrap-up dinner, one of the lead engineers mentioned he had to go back to the office that night to work on a project. I offered, and eventually insisted, that I'd like to go with him. This was a small gesture that signaled my initiative, something I can point to many times over the course of my career and my life that has gotten me to where I am today.

It quickly became apparent that I was going to be a solid performer. I have always been able to solve highly complex problems by distilling them into simple, manageable parts—a skill that has served me well in the worlds of optics, engineering, business, and life in general. I soon became the principal optics guy—and, to their credit, the leaders of the company put a lot of faith in a new guy working on the heart of one of the more complex aspects of the system. They were hard on me—quizzing me on my concepts—but they trusted me. Within three months, I came up with a completely different illumination system. When it came to fruition, they got rewarded.

At the time, I was having a lot of fun in Austin, living it up. Because I was technically a student when I arrived, I was staying at a co-op for the University of Texas for the summer. When the three-month window expired, I decided to delay my PhD. I moved into a house with three roommates. I spent my days working ten to twelve hours, then I'd go downtown, usually getting home after midnight.

Of course, I was a lot younger then.

I emailed the dean of optics at the University of Arizona to let him know of my decision in early August. A week later, I got a large envelope in the mail with what essentially was a three-page burn. The dean said the startup wouldn't make it and that not pursuing my PhD was a mistake.

He was right about one thing: the startup didn't make it. I was one of the last to get let go when it went under. Should I have gotten my PhD? I don't know. We make the best decisions we can at the time with the information available to us, and for me, I did what felt right.

It's not like I didn't have fun while working at the startup. I did. While there, I decided to sign up for kickboxing classes, for example. It wasn't because I thought I'd eventually be a martial artist; it was just a solid step in my quest to hit on more girls in the classes. But the staff saw that I was Asian and somewhat coordinated, so I guess they put some faith in me. It turned out that I got good at it, training five or six days a week.

I mean training for the kickboxing part, not the flirting part.

THE FIRST ANNUAL BONE BRAWL

Would you ever think to take a woman you were dating to something called a Bone Brawl? Would you ever think you would somehow end up in the ring at said Bone Brawl, duct tape in your shorts, fighting a guy you'd never met nicknamed the "Ninja Assassin"? If all this did happen to you, would you believe you would have *still* had to pay fifty dollars to get in to witness your *own* fight?

No?

Well, this is where kickboxing landed me: in the Eddie Deen's Ranch at Downtown Dallas. I'd just taken my date to a nice dinner at the Spaghetti Warehouse, and we'd arrived at the event a bit early. I wanted to support the group of guys from my school fighting that night.

My supposed friend (my kickboxing/grappling teacher) came running up to me all of a sudden, sharing the fantastic news that they had a spot open for their lightweight division. *Why would a guy cancel the night of the fight?* He'd asked if I was in.

"No, no," I told him. "There's no way I'm fighting."

"Dung, you have to help them out," urged my date.

"I don't even have any gear."

"I brought my gear. It's in the trunk," another supposed friend (six foot and change, two-hundred-plus pounds) chimed in, joining the conversation.

"I'm not wearing another man's jockstrap."

I'm in the clear, I thought. *There's no way any of this will fit.*

Another friend—if we can call him that—piped up from the background.

"I've got duct tape!"

Before I knew it, I was in my buddy's shorts—ones that fell below my knees. I went to the prefight conference at 7:45. I met the Ninja Assassin (a buck fifty-five to my buck forty-five). He seemed like a nice guy.

The referee started his spiel. I knew what I was doing in the world of kickboxing in general, but I certainly hadn't been training for any fights. It all felt surreal. I hate wasting food, so if I order something, I clean the plate. I was still full.

"No biting. No elbows. Keep it clean. If your opponent is on the ground, you can't punch him in the face because that's too dangerous," he said as he pointed to the back of his head. "You can put your other hand underneath his head and pound away as much as you want, though. All good?"

What did I get myself into?

"Dude, let's make it simple," I said to my opponent. "Don't hit me in the face here, and I won't hit you in the face. It's obvious I just got roped into this. Plus, I'm on a date."

After the meeting, it was time to get the rest of the gear on. There wasn't a locker room per se in that convention hall, so I walked into a bathroom stall and began to duct tape the cup on. Let's just say that this was a normal convention hall bathroom stall, and not the most well mopped. While the stall was big, I certainly didn't want anything touching the ground. Balancing on one leg, holding my shorts in my mouth and trying to wrap duct tape around my thigh and butt while ensuring that all parts were nicely tucked took a good bit of coordination and energy. Finally, I slipped on the gloves, trying to tighten them around my fingers.

"Hey, you need any help? You alright in there?" my friends said from outside the door.

I was not alright. But I also did not need any help.

"You have to hurry. They are motioning you to the stage."

What the...

As I walked into the hall, still adjusting, I noticed the patrons trying to fill their beer cups before it all started. I didn't blame them.

Then, I heard my name announced.

"Making his way to the stage, Dung..." (Of course, he mispronounced my name.)

What? How am I the first fight of the night?

Having just stepped out of the bathroom, I was escorted to the arena—someone else's mouthpiece in my mouth and all. The spotlights were on me as I stepped into the ring.

One good thing about the timing of it all—from my arrival to being in the ring facing another fighter while wearing duct tape and another man's cup (I don't remember if I'd washed it)—was that it all happened within twenty or thirty minutes. Any of the nervousness a person would normally feel in that situation, I simply didn't have time to feel.

My friend was the coach in the corner of the ring. He put Vaseline on my face, but I didn't know why. He gave me a nod. I nodded back and turned to fight.

Boom. Ninja Assassin kicked me square in the face. I thought it was probably an oversight. Staring into the crowd, the noise became almost inaudible. My peripheral vision started to black out as I took indistinct steps toward just what was in front of me. As my opponent continued to pummel me, I became acutely aware of what "tunnel vision" meant.

Then, he put me in a choke hold, or he tried to. The good thing about that was that I was slippery.

He never got to choke me, and as I moved around, I had time to think. My vision restored. After that, I took him down a couple times.

After the three-minute bell rang, I walked back over to my friend/coach in the corner. I think at first he had been trying to motivate me, but the look on his face at that point said one thing: "Hey, maybe you're actually *not* going to die, dude."

As I turned back to the ring, the adrenaline kicked in. I felt focused. My opponent kicked, and I blocked. Again. Again. I took him down. Once we got into the ground game, I dominated. By the third round, I could hear his coach telling him to stay off the ground. At one point during the round, I had Ninja Assassin in a guillotine choke. Then, I felt him tap my shoulder. I let up, and he spit out his mouthpiece. I thought it was over, but his coach was yelling at him to continue. The referee did not call the fight. I continued to hit the mats around his face after taking him to the ground. After all, we had a deal.

The final bell rang. I was *sure* I'd won. I walked around, blowing kisses to the crowd, arms raised.

When the decision came down, I learned I hadn't won. Why? Because if they were counting punches, he probably did win. I never hit him in the face, even when I clearly could have. They'd missed the tap out.

At the end of the day, I know he and I both knew what happened, and that's all that matters.

As I stepped out of the ring, I shook his hand and said, "Good fight." It took two or three steps before I felt the pain. I could hardly walk because of all the abuse my legs, particularly my shins, had taken. I had felt no pain during the fight, though, besides that initial blow. My adrenaline masked it all.

I hobbled away, and my date had to drive me home. To this day, I can still feel the dents on my shin.

Two years later, I returned to the Bone Brawl, this time as a true spectator, and this time with my now-wife as my date. I watched the guy I fought destroy his opponent in the first round. The Ninja Assassin literally picked his opponent up and slammed his head into the ground. While I did win a stick fighting tournament after the Bone Brawl and did advance a bit more in my training, I knew that my impact on this world would not be made on the mat.

A FLASH OF LOYALTY

We've all heard the story of how Kodak missed the mark, but I lived the story, in a way. The company had one of the first (and some of the best) CCD sensors, or pixelated area light sensors found in many scientific digital cameras today. The problem? They never did anything with the technology back then, instead banking on analog film. They believed box cameras—the disposable kind we all had in the 2000s—

would extend the life of film and be the bridge between the analog and digital worlds. Instead, the digital camera took off too quickly.

Kodak was interested in the technology we had at the startup. They viewed us as having another way to prolong the life of analog film. As one of the technical leaders, I went to Kodak and taught their people about the image station, which is the heart of the digital film processing machine. Kodak had planned to roll out this machine as a faster, cheaper replacement to film developing stations. They were going to manufacturer in Rochester, and I was there to consult and help. During my time there, I was able to learn more about corporate America—about how costs matters to the end customer and, most importantly, how corporate morale can affect productivity.

I made more contacts during that time—which is something that has always helped me professionally, with respect to whatever field I'm in. Because I had access to Nichia LED die through my supply chain connections in Japan—which was nearly impossible to get—I was able to make innovative advancements that changed the game. Even though we met all specs, I continued to innovate and was able to develop an illuminator with Toyoda Gosei die that was more reliable, higher performing, and lower cost than the Nichia Illuminator.

Kodak was interested in our technology as a way to extend

the life of analog film. They were looking for a bit of a rebirth, having gone through years of the "death spiral." I believe they had laid off more than three-quarters of their workforce from a high point in the early eighties.

At the same time, I was recruited by a fast-growing innovative company in the LED world. The head scientist made me a great offer, nearly one and a half times what I was making at the startup. I told the established company that I'd love to take it, but I needed to talk with my team first. I told my boss about the offer, and he was happy for me. He essentially said, "Good luck, and we're going to miss you."

A day later, he came back with a very different response: they were going to match the offer, and they really needed me to stay.

Then, my boss hinted at the prospect that Kodak was going to buy our startup, and they needed a certain retention rate for the deal to go through. Because I was one of the key guys, it was important that I stuck around. Simple as that.

Even though the innovative company was clearly the better and safer opportunity, my loyalty won over. They needed me to stay, so I stayed.

Kodak folded two and a half years later. But hey, it happens. A true reflection of my life is that I can look back at many instances and wonder if I should have made a different choice, but I live life without regret. My path turned out how it did. And I stayed true to myself: as a relationship person, I did what felt right.

Fostering and valuing relationships has played a huge role in my life. It is what made me keep the job at Kodak, but it's also what helped me make all those contacts up and down the supply chain that led to some of the most creative work I've done in my life. There are positives and negatives to every part of us. What we can do is play to our strengths. For me, of course I want to win at things. I want to succeed. But I don't want to win against people I care about. That's not worth it.

It's kind of funny: as my wife really got to know me, she was taken aback by how much more I look out for others' interests over my own. Certainly, I have emotional scars from living this way, but I've also built some pretty amazing relationships over time. A fair trade.

TOWARD THE LIGHT

After Kodak went bust, it was time to look for jobs.

I'd recently met my wife. Because her brothers and her work were close to Dallas, I moved there for the interim. I sent out résumés and got numerous job offers, one of which was for a company in New Jersey. I accepted.

Sitting in the hotel room off of Exit 5 of the Jersey turnpike, frigid winter air outside, I got a call from my soon-to-be partner.

Several months earlier, I'd attended a wedding of an ex-employee from the startup. While there, another colleague and I chatted about my numerous LED ideas. Connections were made.

"Hey, I heard you wanted to start a company. I'm looking to do something in the LED space," my soon-to-be partner said.

He caught me at a good time. I looked out of that crappy hotel window, cold and shivering.

Is this really what I want to do? I wondered.

"I have some ideas I think we can do something with, yeah," I told him. And that was that.

I told the company in New Jersey it wasn't going to work out, and I went back to Dallas. My partner moved his family back to Texas from Maryland, and we got another contact involved too. I started contract work for an optical technologies company in the meantime, but the wheels were turning on the back end. My partners and I had all changed something in our lives and in the lives of our families, on the promise that we'd start this company.

A week after one of my partners moved his family, I got a call from the head scientist at that fast-moving, innovative company. He said he was starting his own company—one that was well-funded, and one that would make me a millionaire within a year. Again, an opportunity.

"My buddy just moved his family to Austin for this," I told him. "It's a great offer. But I just can't."

That was the second big opportunity I passed up, because a year and a half later, that business sold for more than $100 million.

In 2005, my partners and I provided the seed money for our startup, and we developed the first prototypes of our novel LED technology in a partner's garage. In 2007, we got our first Series A round. But none of us had quit our day jobs. I'd taken a *different* day job—one in Austin at a midsize biotech company.

RUMINATIONS AND ILLUMINATIONS

I've always had a skill for reducing complex problems to fundamentals, and my West Point-graduate boss leveraged that in me. There, I was working on equipment to detect bioterror attacks. The detection system was grossly needed, specifically to prevent events like the ones that happened after 9/11, when people were mailing anthrax-filled letters into buildings. We also looked to simplify the more expensive instrumentation and create something more affordable. My role was to build concept design from every aspect—the mechanical and optical system, the industrial design, etc. All of it. And there was one little detail: we needed the POC (proof of concept) finished in about three months. It was a challenge, but we got there.

To validate our POC, we, along with other competing companies, flew to Salt Lake City. After driving a couple of hours to the middle of nowhere, we finally arrived at the military base where the testing was going down. After going through three checkpoints, the companies were each given a trailer. The guys in full bodysuits would bring samples out for us to test, and we had essentially the day to provide results. With our systems, we were able to finish the tasks in very little time. Bored, I walked out of the trailer and started throwing rocks into the distant field. We were in the middle of nowhere, and I was just killing time. At least, I t*hought* I was—that is, until several soldiers showed up and "kindly" asked me to stop because I was throwing rocks at potential mines. In fact, they explained, we were in the middle of a minefield. (AWESOME.)

At the time, I was also working on a project to pitch to the Bill & Melinda Gates Foundation to address their edict of preventing the next pandemic. I was developing a miniature version of my employer's core instrumentation. The goal was to develop a handheld diagnostics instrument that could test and identify what strain of respiratory illness a person may have contracted. (Again, this would be extremely helpful today in the era of COVID-19. As we've all learned during COVID-19, testing is paramount to being able to identify, isolate, contact trace, and continue the economy.)

We were pitching the idea to the Bill & Melinda Gates Foundation because we needed funding and support to bring the technology to market. At the same time, my partners and I got our Series B round of funding. Though we'd had the company for years, none of us had taken any salary yet. We'd only hired two employees—so employee number one was not even one of the founders. With the Series B, it became apparent that if we were going to move forward, we needed to go all in. No part-time stuff. We'd worked hard to get to this point and were ready to go.

I was torn. My passion has always been to find and fund technology that helps the world, and a handheld diagnostic instrument would do that. But so would the energy-saving LED technology we'd built (literally in a garage). Some thought it would be an easy decision to jump out on my own, but it wasn't. I definitely had to think about it. In the end, some relationship pieces weren't fitting for me at my current employer.

After a little less than a year, I left the biotech company for my own. While still around, the company I started is no longer the same. I went on to help start another, which got sold. In each endeavor, I'm proud to have been a part of the formation of technologies to improve the world. It's been a journey of ups and downs, but—like I said—I have no regrets.

I've always played the hand I had as best I could.

chapter / two

ON A MISSION

Vietnam, 1979. Nobody has seen us, and we board the larger ship as planned. There are twenty or thirty people on the fishing boat. My uncle is there too, the one with an extra thumb on one of his hands. We are all crammed together. We see land and are hopeful. But soon, the winds shift.

* * *

I walked into my admissions interview at MIT looking like I'd entered a wet T-shirt contest.

The recruiter wanted to interview me in his office, so I'd made the trek to Crystal City. Already an hour late having fought DC traffic, I got out of my car and stepped into the pouring rain. Of course, I did not have an umbrella. Of course, when I finally made it into his office, it was very cold in there. I'm not going to spell the rest out for you.

I'm not sure that interviewer liked me much. I probably wouldn't have liked me much. I didn't get in to MIT.

As my high school graduation approached, everyone had said to apply to four schools: two safe ones, one you truly want, and one long shot. For most of the colleges on my list—Virginia Tech, UVA, Stanford, Duke, and others—their application packets were thick. I was definitely contemplating going to an out-of-state school, as I wasn't getting along with my dad that well at the time.

One day, I saw a flyer for Rose-Hulman Institute of Technology. The flyer mentioned they were consistently one of *U.S. News & World Report*'s top-ranking engineering schools. It looked interesting—even though it was in Indiana, somewhere I'd never been.

What stuck out about Rose, to me, was also what they *didn't* have: the hassle. Their application was a one-pager, and the application fee was reasonable. Soon after, I got a visit from a recruiter. He offered me a scholarship, and I took it. Decision made, and it all started with that one flyer.

One thing the recruiter never mentioned, though, was that Rose was an all-male school at the time. (Women wouldn't be admitted until one year later. Should have visited the campus prior to committing.)

So, it was then I started my college experience as the only Asian in my small, dude-filled class, smack in the middle of Indiana.

SENIOR SHENANIGANS

On campus, I was known as the guy who was always wearing shorts, usually walking back from the dining hall with an ice cream cone in hand. That was true whether it was summer or we had one foot of snow on the ground. I also played sports with my roommates, always doing push-ups before games and wearing a black turtleneck when I played basketball.

Don't ask me why. I just did. Picture a short Asian wearing a black turtleneck in cornfield Indiana playing basketball. At least it's not spandex?

Our intramural teams were excellent, and the group of friends I surrounded myself with were, let's just say…a varied bunch. For example, we had a quick-witted offensive lineman who was always ready for a game (cards, sports, drinking, whatever). There was my freshman roommate, whose emotions were tied too heavily to academic performance. There was my best friend, whose stories were (and are) always bigger and better than the next person's...just because. There was my adopted buddy who had the traditional requisite trappings of popularity, but marched to a different beat. There was "Woman"—yes, her nickname—who was one of eight consortium women admitted to Rose my freshman year. She was the practical, calming voice that gave us the competitive edge in co-ed intramural leagues. And then there was me: yeah, so I occasionally dabbled in Dungeons & Dragons, but I could also spike a volleyball (on a very good day, with maybe an under-tolerance net height).

All told, as the Asian guy in the freshman class who also did weird things, I stood out, whether good or bad. I was a leader on the Student Activities Board (SAB) and became the president my senior year. SAB is in charge of scheduling concerts and events on campus. We were one of the first places to book Jeff Dunham, and grabbing a beer after with him was great. My all-time favorite act was a singer/comedian turned motivational speaker, Mike Rayburn. He was talented, funny, different, a little crazy, and inspirational. We hired him every year I was at Rose.

My activities on campus continued even outside of SAB, where I was a member of the disciplinary crew. I knew many of the administrators, and I was proud to be asked to student teach an optics class. (Because Rose does not offer a PhD in engineering, student teaching wasn't the norm.)

All that said, I was known on campus by students and faculty, whether it was because they thought I was weird, I hooked them up with a good show, or they needed a hand academically.

As senior year was coming to an end, we knew one thing had to be done. We had to get a prank in before graduation. I'd heard it had been done by previous classes, and some students had gotten expelled. But I was confident we would be fine. I invited the student leaders on campus, including the RAs, to join our mission, and I started organizing meetings.

If you ever want to hear a bunch of crazy prank ideas, gather a room full of engineering students who are about to be set free into the world.

One idea came up repeatedly: we all wanted to prank a mean-as-hell professor whose tenure afforded him the power of Satan from the mechanical engineering department. And for good reason.

Of all the years I was at Rose, my best friend and I had never had a class together. I studied optical engineering, and we both studied mechanical engineering. I say our paths never crossed in class because I was always taking classes a year ahead of him, having opted to pursue two degrees. But if you asked him today, he'd have a different and better story, I'm sure.

All that changed first trimester of our senior year: the class was Vibrations. Of course, we couldn't miss the opportunity to see which one of us measured up.

We'd long been competitive academically, in fact. And we lived together, so we knew each other's strengths and weaknesses. He always had a better GPA than I did. I had a 3.5 at the time, and he'd only gotten one B his entire college career. (I'd say his GPA started to slip a little when we started living together.) He was always the big drinker, but he needed a venue and someone who could hang. I have to admit that I really didn't drink before college. That changed. But that's another story.

The mechanical engineering professor was a round man with a small neck, and some students called him Turtle Man (Dr. T for short). He was tenured, and also very mean. I'd heard stories of him making students cry simply because of his demeanor and tearing homework up in the face of the person trying to turn it in. Needless to say, in our vibrations class, there was no partial credit, no nothing.

My friend and I knew we were both going to ace the class, so we had our own competition: to see who could do the absolute least amount of work and still get an A. I figured he'd win because he has always been the top dog academically. To this day, it is crazy how smart he is.

The first day of class, Dr. T. told us he would grade no homework. Instead, our final grade would be determined only by ten quizzes and a final. My eyes lit up when I heard that. With that type of system, I thought maybe I had a shot. I rarely did homework in college anyway, so the setup was right up my alley.

And it was. I got the highest grade that trimester. More than that, though, Dr. T. was personable with me and recommended me for a shock and vibrations internship at Los Alamos National Laboratory.

Similarly, I also got along well with another no-nonsense professor who taught upper-level optics classes. He was also a tenured teacher, and people shied away from him. I did not. Once, when we were doing a holography experiment in class, he spilled one of the film development chemicals because he was juggling so many of them. (Some of these development chemicals are not so nice, by the way.)

The class stood there and watched as the professor continued to struggle to get everything ready. I grabbed some sheets of paper and got on my hands and knees, wiping the spill. It wasn't that I was trying to show off, and I didn't think my reaction was strange until I looked back at my classmates, who still hadn't moved. I made a joke about them pitching in, and they started to.

As much as I kid around, I have always gotten along with my professors. My Vietnamese parents taught me to hold teachers with the highest respect. Consciously or subconsciously, this is my guiding star when dealing with people in general. That strategy has helped me throughout my life—approaching people as people, no matter what title they have. At the end of the day, some of the downright grittiest guys have been my biggest advocates.

Back to the prank. You can see now why pranking Dr. T. sounded like a good idea. Some in the group wanted to take the professor's Harley (yes, he drove a Harley) and put it on a floating platform in the lake on campus. Others wanted to steal the bike, dismantle it piece by piece, and reassemble it on a rooftop on campus.

We didn't steal the bike. I think that's a good thing because that might have gotten us expelled.

We decided that we needed to get back at campus security. It was the first year they'd started putting the boot on cars, and my coconspirators had gotten the boot quite a bit. At the time, there were several changes at Rose. They were starting to make headway in expanding their facilities: a new gym was opened, new buildings were opening up, and construction equipment was everywhere. I thought it was the biggest gym I'd ever seen in my entire life. When I go back now, it seems so small. Everything is different when you look back at it.

We did get back at security—but they got us too.

We'd also decided to remove all the light bulbs in one of the halls. The three-story building did not have windows, so it would be pitch black. I was one of the guys who took a ladder there at night, starting to unscrew light bulbs in every classroom on every floor. It was a group effort. My friends and I had gotten about halfway done, then everybody suddenly scattered.

We'd been spotted by security—who certainly didn't know what we were up to, because it was dark outside (and now inside). But they knew enough to yell for us to stop.

We all booked it out of there.

I headed to another hall, the place I'd told everyone to convene if anything happened. As I counted heads, I realized we were missing someone: it was Squid, my friend who'd had one leg amputated as a child and now walked with crutches. We affectionately referred to him as "Squid," a nickname he approved. *Squid is the fastest out of all of us, even on crutches*, I thought. *Where is he?*

I leave no man behind.

I led the group back to the now-dark hall, where we were—not surprisingly—met by security.

"You kids had better put all this back or we will need to call the real cops," security said.

We did what he said, sort of. When I found Squid, I had to know what happened.

"Dude, why didn't you run?" I asked him.

"Yeah, look at me," he said. "I know I'm fast. But it's not like he can't pick me out of a lineup."

"That's a pretty good point."

In the end, our prank was multifaceted: we also changed every clock in another building, one sure to cause commotion. Because Rose was still on a bell system, that meant people were milling around after a bell, unsure of what time it was or where to go next. There was a flower bed in front of that hall that spelled "RHIT" in flowers. We thought about changing the first letter, but decided that would have definitely gotten us expelled. So, we bought limestone and wrote "'98 rules" to cover it instead.

None of that topped our biggest prank: we stole a security car and drove it to the middle of the quadrangle at Rose.

There, we booted it and covered the windshield in soap, leaving a note that said we'd give the keys back at noon.

The entire endeavor was well-orchestrated from the students in the mail room to the newspaper, and word got out. An article of the event was published that had pictures of the security car. By the time it was time to hand back the keys, I didn't even go. I was tired, having not had many all-nighters. At seven that morning, I finally went to sleep, thinking we'd successfully pulled everything off anonymously.

I was wrong about the anonymous part.

I finally got to campus that afternoon. Senior year, classes were mostly optional. Hopefully, my former professors aren't reading this. (Especially the professor whose class I only attended seven times—the first day, three test days, senior presentation day, the last day, and the final.) I checked my mail locker as I usually do, and I found a note. It read, "The president would like to see you at this time."

What do I say now? I thought. *And who spilled the beans?*

The president—who was a great guy and has since unfortunately passed away—called four people, including me, into his office. We were the ringleaders, and he knew it. Before he called us in, he made us wait in the lobby for half an hour—for added tension, surely.

It worked. I was nervous. I knew I'd had harmless fun, but I wondered if one of the other guys went overboard.

As soon as we walked in, the president stared us down with a serious look on his face. He walked around his desk, sighing animatedly. As he sat back in his chair, a big smile came on his face.

"Well done, guys," he said. "Way not to be destructive. The lime will wash away. Even the kind of paint you used was well thought-out."

(He was right. We'd gone with water soluble paint so it wouldn't stick.)

"All I want you to do is take back the challenge to the next class."

He was talking about an article we'd planned to publish that would, indeed, challenge the next class to do better when they did their prank.

We, of course, rescinded it and followed his instruction. And nobody got expelled.

THE 'MAN' IN UNDERCLASSMAN

My sophomore year of college, I decided to add a mechanical engineering degree to the applied optics degree (having already changed from electrical engineering when I first enrolled). Never the one to shy away from a challenge, I recall studying the course schedule and recognizing that I could fit in an extra degree instead of just another major. The field of optics was pretty obscure, sort of the fries in the "would you like fries with that" version of engineering. I wanted to make sure I would have access to opportunities when I graduated. What solidified my decision was when my advisor gave me one piece of advice: "Dung, it doesn't really matter what you choose. As long as you're good at it, there will be a job for you...well, geographically it might not be the *best* place, but there will be a job somewhere."

Geographically? What?

That alone was enough to convince me: I pursued a second degree in mechanical engineering.

From that point forward, my average course load was twenty hours a trimester. Between all my classes and my campus activities, I was on campus almost all the time. My fraternity house, Pike House, was *not* on campus, so many nights I found myself walking the few miles home.

Because I wasn't around often—and because I wasn't in the same classes as any of my fraternity brothers—I didn't get super close with a lot of them. There are a lot of good guys in Pike, and especially in my class. There was Squid—the guy who was fast even on crutches. Another of my friends, a short, chubby guy from the Philippines, who was excellent at playing the piano. We all came into a fraternity with different expectations. There certainly were full-of-personality, fun-loving, partying, normal dudes who would venture to the middle of nowhere for an engineering education. I was closer to a few of them. Overall, though, I did not fit in, feeling more comfortable at the outer edges.

I also made friends with the GDI guys—the Gamma Delta Iotas (or the God Damn Independents, as they called themselves)—who didn't join Greek life. This included my best bud, of course—who couldn't get into a fraternity if he tried. (And I can say that because he's still my friend.) The GDI guys got me into playing Dungeons & Dragons a few times that year—the nerdiest of nerdy ways to spend your time. I never got into it like they did, but I'd be lying if I said I didn't spend some Friday and Saturday nights that way.

Go ahead—judge away. There's a stigma around Dungeons & Dragons, and as someone who dabbled in it for a year, I can tell you one thing: it's probably true.

My junior year, I remained in the fraternity but moved out of the Pike house and into an apartment at Village Quarters, about five miles away from Rose. It was a three-bedroom apartment, but we always had six, if not seven, guys in the apartment. In total, there were never fewer than ten people there at one time.

(I'll let you do that math.)

Living at Village Quarters, privacy was not my friend. I've walked in on my roommates doing things that are now burned into my brain. I can never get them out.

Because we were engineers, we'd calculate random facts about our living situation: the amount of sewage we would go through in that place in a month was the volume of the apartment's living room. Our liquor cabinet was worth more than a month's rent. The list goes on.

It was—eh—a collection of interesting guys and interesting experiences. It worked for me, though, because I have always been the kind of guy who goes with the flow in situations and makes friends with everyone, especially those who are a little outside of the norm.

ATTACK OF THE WINDOW SCREEN

We didn't have much by way of fancy furniture during those years. We had mattresses on the floor, and I'd bought a single futon.

I still have that $150 futon somewhere. Or at least I think I do, unless my wife has gotten rid of it behind my back.

One party in the apartment ended memorably, in a chilly way. We would gather there a lot, and women from St. Mary's would come over. One night, my girlfriend and I went back to my room. It was so hot in that room due to the heater and small space. So, even in midwinter Indiana, we opened the window. We cozied up, of course. That's always nice, right?

I always shower before I fall asleep, so I did that, postcuddle. I hopped back into bed and covered with the blanket, freezing by that time. We were both drinking at the party, naturally, so we didn't think to close the window before we fell asleep.

The next morning, I woke up shivering. But I had a bigger problem: I tried to move to shut the window, but I couldn't. I was stuck. Though I couldn't see her face, I figured my girlfriend must have been looking at me in a weird way. One of my roommates walked into the room, and I heard something I never thought I'd hear:

"Dude, you're frozen to the window."

I figured it out: after my shower, my wet hair had gotten in the window screen. There I was, a half-naked guy, stuck to my own window.

My friends laughed and left me there, being the good friends they were. I can't remember who eventually brought me warm water—hopefully it was my girlfriend, but who knows—to unstick me.

It was not my proudest moment.

MAKING CONNECTIONS AT SAB

They say what happens to you in college is what ultimately happens to you in life, and that is mostly true, in my experience. I made the most of my time there. I grew a lot in my understanding of mixing the social, academic, and leadership pieces of life—and how to deal with them together. I honed my ability to get the best out of people and make their lives richer. Mine got richer for it too.

SAB (Student Activities Board), for instance, was not popular on campus. There were few members, and unfortunately, retention rate was fairly low. Like everything I venture into, it took me some time to assess the club and become a vocal member. I became the promotions chair that year—probably more due to a lack of bodies than my leadership talent. By my senior year, I was president, having rewritten SAB's constitution. By the time I left, we had grown the budget, increased membership, and sponsored many well-attended activities.

In 2018, I went back for my twenty-year reunion, and more than half of the people there were from SAB. It was a good feeling, seeing I'd made a lasting impact on people and hearing how they were doing. Obviously, I didn't always go with the norm in school. I followed my own path. And in the end, we'd all learned from each other.

At my time in SAB, I learned that leadership matters, as does the foundation of a club (or organization). I had to change both before I became president, which is why I rewrote the constitution. It's hard enough to pay people to do something, but it's even harder to convince time-constrained, academically-focused kids to volunteer their valuable time for the betterment of campus life. I recognized that all I had to offer (besides a résumé boost) was a feeling of belonging, a fun time, and empowerment. Their voices mattered in what the whole campus would see and do for several hours a month. Back then, I also coerced my roommates to participate. Though not the volunteering types, I think they had fun. (I know they'd dispute that, but this is *my* book.)

At the end of the day—then and throughout my life—I've found that people will inherently do better and be better if given the opportunity to do so by those genuinely interested in lifting them up.

RUMINATIONS AND ILLUMINATIONS

This philosophy extends far beyond SAB. I have lifted my wife up, too, in a way, though she would never admit it. Because she didn't arrive in the US until she was nineteen, she'd always believed there was a ceiling to what she could do here in terms of her advancement and earning potential. She knows she is a great individual contributor and can manage a small group of people, but having "just OK" English has, in the past, made her question whether she'd be able to get her ideas across in front of large groups. It was a resignation of sorts, and it's one I definitely have never reinforced.

I have heard a common refrain in the voices of many people I talk to who have faced an immigration situation: they think, "Dung, you were born here. Of *course* this is easy for you."

The best thing I can do in those situations is talk about people other than myself. I often tell my wife about one person I hired at a high salary. He was a brilliant scientist, and I knew he had expertise in a specific area my company needed. I also could not understand hardly anything he said; he had worse than "just OK" English. But I was willing to pay that to have access to his talent. The challenge, then, was *mine*—not his. I had to learn to understand what he was communicating. He was giving me the golden nugget of information I needed, and my job was to find out how to get it.

I don't believe in ceilings, and I don't believe in using anything as a crutch. Now, of course there are physical limits to things we can do. But other than that, don't tell me there's an insurmountable hurdle. There is a way. I have been in some very dark places in my life, and I've come out of them. There is always a way.

Today, I don't believe my wife sees hurdles anymore. She is climbing the ladder. I always tell her she's a much better leader than I am, for two reasons: she needs to hear it, and it's true.

Another reason I don't believe in ceilings is my own experience. I arrived at Rose-Hulman socially inept, academically beaten down, low-esteemed, and lost. I had run away from Northern Virginia, joined a fraternity to fit in, and found solace in a group of guys that did not quite belong to their respective stereotypes. And yet, we made an impact and left Rose better than the day we arrived.

My college years and before, I have moved through the world not necessarily caring what people thought of me. I have been friendly to everyone and goal-focused always, even as a disarmingly weird guy in the middle of Indiana. Even though it may not feel that way sometimes, there *is* a way—even if you have to make it yourself.

So far, as we've Benjamin Button-ed our way through my

story, you've seen many of my high cards. As we move forward, the deck starts to look a little different.

chapter / *three*

DARKER DAYS

Vietnam, 1979. *We begin to move away from the land, not toward it. The adults are saying something has gone wrong with the motor. We are at the mercy of the sea. We are stranded, waves reaching the horizon from every viewpoint.*

* * *

High school was challenging for me. In my earlier school years, I was the top dog as far as academics. At Thomas Jefferson High School for Science and Technology (TJ), the top magnet school in the country, I was no longer at the top of anything. Before, although I was always smaller than most of my classmates, I could keep up and even excel athletically. That also was not the case at TJ.

I mentioned I've been in a dark place before, and these

years hold one of those moments for me. My sister left for college in Charlottesville. She had always been my go-to person—and is today, still. That meant I was home with my parents solo, and my father and I did not get along much.

We argued frequently. I wouldn't say I had a great home life, but I had nowhere else to go. I didn't have money to go to the mall or drive anywhere for fun. Certainly, my dad's life was just as reclusive as mine, if not more so. His main hobby was gardening, building things like decks and gazebos, and going to thrift shops. Because of his vision problems, I was his escape from life. When we spent time together, that's often what we did—build things, grow things. He'd nitpick my work, but I was used to it.

As soon as I could drive, I was constantly taking him to Hechinger, Home Depot, or other supply stores so he could spend what little money we had on building material. I also took my dad—who could not drive because he'd lost much of his vision—to thrift stores, a pastime he enjoyed. He'd put me down consistently through it all. I knew even then that my intellectual capacity was definitely beyond that of my parents. Maybe he knew it too. I did everything technical or advanced in the house—hooking up electronics and the like. My dad, in his own right, was highly intelligent. In Vietnam, citizens take a national test that ranks intelligence, and he placed second in the entire country when he took it. But in the US, with the language barrier, his age, and his loss of vision, things no longer came easy for him. In reality, everything was difficult for him.

It was also painfully obvious to anyone looking that we were far more impoverished than any of my mom's siblings. I believe they looked down on my family, and he didn't take it well. My dad grew up very poor; my grandmother sold soup on the street corner so her kids could survive. My grandfather was never around, so my dad assumed the patriarchal role of the family, caring for his brother and three sisters. He had another brother, who died in the war. He started to work at an early age. With his intellect, he was able to make money tutoring. He climbed a steep ladder, married into an affluent family, and attained recognition; he was at the pinnacle of success. Then, communism took over.

Immigrating to the US was a big change for him culturally, but the bigger change was that he was no longer in control. Whereas before people depended on him and needed him, this was a new reality: he needed us as much as we needed him. Unfortunately, with few other options, he took it out on me.

I want to be very clear: he never abused us physically, never once hit us. It was all emotional. It affected both my sister and I, but in the end, maybe that's what made us tougher.

My relationship with my father was already quite poor, but

one incident in particular was the proverbial straw that broke the camel's back. Our relationship never recovered after it. He has mellowed in his later years, and my sister is the glue that holds us together. That's fitting, because she was also there for our unbinding.

Once, my sister called from UVA and mentioned that she didn't have any comfortable chairs in her dorm. Academically, she felt she was also struggling a little because she could not concentrate—which, in my prideful Asian family, always meant getting less than A's. There was a shame associated with that, one we didn't choose but was there nonetheless. My sister is smart. She was the valedictorian of her class at Falls Church High School. (She doesn't think I'm proud of her for this, but I always have been.) I didn't like that she was having a hard time.

I qualified for reduced lunches at TJ, and my parents gave me an allowance of a couple dollars a day to pay for food. Scrawny as I was, I decided I simply wouldn't eat and would save the ten dollars a week until I could get her a chair. (Even then, I had strong willpower. Once you've gone seven days without food, it's easy to go without a lot of essentials.) I found it: a chair and matching ottoman from Montgomery Ward, on sale for $150. I wanted to get it for her, so I did.

I was proud, and my sister was grateful. But my dad had

the opposite reaction. I'd apparently further exposed that he was no longer in control, not choosing to or being able to get it for her himself. He and I got into a big fight, to put it mildly. I'm a person who will tolerate a lot of things, but if someone does something that is not congruent to what a situation calls for, if they go too far, I have a hard time forgiving them. That stands today.

That day, I stormed out of the house without even taking time to put on shoes, and drove. I was pissed, and I felt on edge. I headed to the cemetery and drove around, thinking about things I shouldn't have. I thought of my father and wondered if that was my future, finding whatever job I could and going to thrift stores, mad at the world.

Even though he never said it, I think he genuinely felt bad about what happened. He took the next couple days off work after it happened, staying in bed. I never told him about the cemetery or the reason that was my symbolic place to lament about the situation.

FALL FROM GRACE

I'm not sure how it is now, but back then, getting into TJ wasn't easy. My teacher at Luther Jackson Middle School recommended me along with a couple other students. The entrance testing was rather grueling. I remember an eight-hour test split into two sections. I was required to get teacher recommendations, write an essay, and complete a long application.

My middle school was in a tough neighborhood, and I had long been an academic overachiever. I knew TJ was the best school; when the opportunity presented itself, I jumped through all the hoops. I wanted the challenge.

Because TJ was a magnet school, we had to start our days at our base high school. That meant I'd take a bus to Falls Church High School (also not in the best of neighborhoods), then another one to TJ. This presented a semisegregation on the social scale. Imagine a group of nerdy kids are waiting for a bus to take them to another high school, while other kids their age walk past. You can envision the jeering, I'm sure. It also bonded our small group, though. It wasn't all bad; we still had fun.

I felt mediocre at best compared to my elite TJ classmates. Most of the students were from affluent, or at least middle class, neighborhoods. My parents were barely scraping by. I weighed barely one hundred pounds. I had no transportation and little money. That meant intramural sports, clubs, and social gatherings were not part of my high school experience.

I was in the middle academically too. To give you an idea, my class of 400 students had over 100 National Merit

Scholars. One of my friends hacked into the Department of Defense (DOD), just to prove he could. Another person from class *already* had a business buying/selling real estate in DC. We had a self-made millionaire, a *Jeopardy!* champion, and a lot of very talented and accomplished teens.

And me? I felt like a fish out of water. Even mathematics, which always came easily to me, presented a challenge. I'd won the French award in middle school, excelling. I got my first C in French at TJ. I was in the chess club, but got completely outplayed by a fellow student who was playing me and nine others at the same time. At one point, I started wearing all black and hanging around theater people, not sure of where I fit in anywhere else.

It wasn't just school. I was also dealing with teenager struggles, having the rollercoasters of emotion. Girls I thought were cute didn't want to talk to me, even though I tried. I felt small, physically and emotionally, and my confidence suffered. It was a smack in the face: all these things that once had been extraordinarily easy became difficult.

During this time, I also struggled with something I have grappled with often in my life, and maybe always will: the pull between my Vietnamese side and my Western side. In reality, I have always gotten along better with Westerners. I feel more comfortable there. And I'd never had to try to feel comfortable before high school—I just *did*. At TJ, I did have to try, and I failed. I never felt like I was good enough, and that was painful in a lot of ways. That, coupled with challenges at home, made high school a rough time in my life.

LASER COOLING IS COOL, TRUST ME

My junior and senior years at TJ were certainly better than the first two. I'd settled in a bit. At TJ, you had to select a senior research project. I chose the optics lab with a professor I admired and began my research on a boundary-pushing topic in the field: laser cooling.

Laser cooling is a method of creating an optical potential well to hold an atom in place. When an atom is stationary, it has zero kinetic energy and is at absolute zero. Look, it's cool, OK? Not nerdy at all, according to a nerd.

Despite my family's financial situation, there was no question in their minds or mine that I was going to college. I knew I needed to get as many scholarships as I could, so I dove headlong into laser cooling and the quest for absolute zero. Spoiler alert: to this day, no one has reached absolute zero. It's almost an impossibility. Which, to me, has always meant it's still a little possible.

The end of my junior year and that summer, I spent much of my time in various libraries. I even drove to UVA several times to find more obscure journals and books on the topic.

For my project, I followed the work of Carl Wieman from the University of Colorado. He has since won a Nobel Prize. I also followed the work of Steven Chu, who has also won a Nobel Prize for laser cooling.

I had my research. My professor bought the supplies. I started with one laser selected to output at approximately the resonance frequency of cesium. I would then tune it using a thermoelectric cooler to shift it slightly off the resonant frequency.

The end result would be combining six lasers pointed at each other to create the optical potential well. They were all trying to push the atoms toward the center and hold them there.

This is cool, remember?

It would have been cooler if I'd won the Westinghouse Award, which I didn't. But I *did* get a participation award (don't get me started on those) and a full scholarship to attend George Washington from one of the judges. I was grateful for the offer, but at the time, I'd already been accepted to Rose.

It was set: absolute zero was still elusive, and I was on a path to Indiana.

EMOTIONAL NEUTRALITY: ANOTHER ABSOLUTE ZERO

In Vietnamese culture, we are taught to respect our elders. That is inherently a part of me. I realize there's a lot of confidence a guy like me should have that I don't. I lost that growing up. Because I didn't have any deep connections at home, I was very guarded in all my relationships. I will tell you what happened, but it's different in terms of communicating how I feel about it. I generally avoid those conversations and try to laugh them off instead. This hasn't gone away with age. I think even my wife would say I'm guarded and cold.

I realize this about myself, though. I don't hide it. I'm actually fascinated by psychology and the study of our minds, and while I've never been to therapy, I've spent much of my life borderline obsessively introspecting.

The good thing about being relatively emotionally neutral is that it is easy for people to feel comfortable with me, and it's easy to start a conversation and joke around. Some (OK, most) would say that my jokes are bad, but c'est la vie. I approach relationships with a sort of distance, but one that is inviting and open. I'm always a bit more willing to fight when the moral and ethical lines are not blurred but well-crossed. But for the most part, I have had enough conflicts in my life that I am OK with shielding myself from it when possible.

It's *not* possible sometimes. That's the world we live in.

The good news is that, because of the toughness I learned as a kid and even at TJ, I am morally grounded. I always know what side I'm on, and I respect what side you're on. I don't want to fight about it, and I especially don't want to hurt anyone's feelings. I have a deep emotional avoidance to hurting someone's feelings or putting people down, and sometimes that means making a joke or changing the subject.

The exception is when I know you really well, then it's an all-out teasing war. Strong shield, but it can be broken.

RUMINATIONS AND ILLUMINATIONS

There have been many circumstances in my life where those around me thought the world was imploding. My nature is to thrive in those situations. To problem-solve. To figure out the solution and make the best of the situation. As an adult, I've noted specifically that my leadership comes out in the most challenging of times.

I have a calmness in chaos and ability to push forward no matter the circumstances. Is that a result of experiences in my life that have forced me to stare death in the eyes? I don't know. But I do know it's served me well, as has my ability to think independently and critically about big questions, simplifying them to their foundational elements. I tell people that I am not smart enough to deal with the complex; it's much easier to solve the fundamentally simple problems.

I learned something during these challenging in-between high school years (and before), whether I knew I was learning it at the time or not: at the end of the day, I know the only person I can ever rely on is myself. Having to rely on another person entirely—in business, in life—is a risk. It's a chance to be disappointed. The only person I've ever fully trusted is me. The way I look at it is simple: few people know who I am, so how am I ever going to know anyone else? That's why I keep to myself and don't judge people. Judging requires that I know and understand how the world works, which I don't. I am not religious. I can only live my life, and until other lives affect mine, I try not to interfere.

This, again, comes back to the Eastern and Western sides of me. From the start, I've known the world is only so big. I've known I wanted to help. I wanted to do something above the trivialities of much of what we go through daily. That has fortified my shield, which can come off as coldness. But it's a necessary coldness. These are not things you can do meekly.

The highest degree of self-reliance can be a lonely place. I admit that. I know what works for me won't work for other people, and some may even find my approach detrimental. But that all goes back to the high value I place on independence. We must know ourselves well enough to be able to navigate the world with the skills we have. Maybe where I have coldness, you have warmth. As long as they're working for us, respectively, we are not wrong.

I don't wish coldness for my children. They will have their own issues to deal with in life. If I could shield them from what is hard, I would. But that is not possible, and the self-reliance they need to overcome those hard moments is what I worry they are too coddled to form. That's why I wrote this book, at the end of the day. For them. And for you too. So, when you forget to or are unable to steel yourself against your challenges, you will remember that there's always a light. If you don't see the light at first, look at it a different way.

chapter / *four*

COMING OF AGE

Vietnam, 1979. *Once, amid the drifting, we hit a floating island and spend the night there. It is so cold on the island that we all have to huddle together...the kids on the inside, then women, then men on the outside. It is hard to walk back to the boat the next day because the tide is coming in. One man who had been seasick got off the boat, but I don't see him get back on with us.*

* * *

Seventh grade is the year I got beat up by a group of elementary kids. That's as good a way to start this off as any, right?

(This is where I discovered, once and for all, that maybe I'd never be a physical superstar.)

It happened when I was walking home from the bus stop I used to get to and from Luther Jackson. We'd just moved out of our three-bedroom townhouse into a house approximately a mile down the road. Even though we had moved across a major road and there were bus stops closer to my new home, I still made the trek back across the street to Kingsley Commons.

My family and I had stayed in one bedroom of the townhouse and had rented out the others. That, or we had other family members there. We had people sleeping on the couches, in the dining room area—wherever we could fit bodies.

One renter at the townhouse was a twentysomething young man who made quite an impression on me. I wouldn't say he was a gangster, but I would say his reputation wasn't that of a choirboy. I never found out what he did for work. He always had a knife with him, and he wore a punkish pocket chain. I heard stories of him pouring sugar into people's gasoline tanks, and he'd coordinate and participate in races down Route 50 from DC—which had multiple stoplights—with the goal of not stopping for any of them.

Despite all that, I was never scared of him. He was a decent guy, and he was my friend. Sometimes, when my parents were at work, he'd let me watch him sharpen his bowie knife and even let me hold it. I felt very cool.

His living with us there in the townhouse helped everyone—we were able to afford the rent, and he got to be around a bit of our family life. Sure, my parents argued all the time, and we struggled financially, but I wonder if seeing our family showed him something he had been missing. We'd later learn that having him live with us actually protected us from the gangs, not the other way around. He'd told them not to mess with us. My instincts about him were right: he *was* good. After he left, we kept in touch. He became a businessman and now has a family.

The townhouse was the most luxurious place I'd ever experienced, even though it was small and cockroach-infested. But it was better than living under a car, or on an island. I had a mattress. And I had a roommate. I have never looked at any of these experiences in my life as overtly negative: they were just my experiences.

We left the townhouse, again, when my parents bought a house nearby—a dilapidated 1950s-era, 800-square-foot home—which was, again, cockroach-infested. Before moving in, we had secured renters for the basement. As part of the deal, the new renter (a carpenter by trade) would turn the basement into a three-bedroom floor that mirrored the upper level. We also had a renter for one of the bedrooms upstairs. My sister and I still contributed by collating and stamping mail when there were overflow projects at my mom's workplace. At the time, it seemed like there was always overflow work. Even so, my parents worked constantly—my mom at a mail shop, and my dad repairing toilets and air conditioners as a maintenance man.

It was returning to that house—again, headed home from the bus stop—that I got attacked by elementary kids.

The three kids had walked out of a 7-Eleven, and they approached me to ask if I had a quarter. I, of course, did not have a quarter (or any money). I tried to walk away, but they started punching me, all of them. Whaling on me. I didn't fight back and instead continued to walk home, with them still hitting me all the way.

I had some bruises and a black eye, and my parents even called the cops. Nothing consequential ever came from it, and I continued to walk up and down that street to the bus stop every day till that school year ended. Every once in a while, I'd see the kids who lived there at Kingsley Commons. I knew the area because it was where our townhome was located.

Looking back, that was my first experience with violence associated with poverty. I never knew their situations or home lives, obviously, but I had lived in Kingsley Commons too. In some ways, the incident genuinely didn't bother me much because I understood the poverty, the instability, the feeling of having/being nothing. That might be why I never hit them back. Not that it justifies what they did, but at the time, I mostly felt sorry for them. I couldn't do anything to change it, so it became a nonevent to me.

That's my ability to roll with the punches, I guess you could say.

MAKING ENDS MEET

My dad had a mechanical engineering background in Vietnam, but due to his declining vision, he was not able to do much of the work he used to do when we got to the US. His vision was so poor that he once rear-ended a white car parked at a stop light in our Pinto, and when we asked what happened, he said he did not see it. We later discovered that was because the taillights were not on, which would signal to my dad that the car was there. Even so, he continued to drive; there was no other option. The good news is that he only got into three total wrecks (all minor). The bad news is that I am sure him driving all over the NoVA-DC-Maryland area did not help the Asian driving stereotypes. His role as a facilities manager, repairing and maintaining equipment in a government building, is where he spent most of his time. He stopped driving when he got a more permanent position in DC for two reasons: first, let's be honest, no one wants to drive in DC. Plus, it was more cost-effective to use mass transit.

My mom had relatively good employers in the mail shop.

She quickly rose through the ranks because she was hardworking, and she adapted her skills rapidly. She'd eventually run the automated machines and become a supervisor.

My mom's professional strengths have always been her business acumen, her ability to remember numbers and do basic math, and her competitive fire. If you did business with her, she could look at you and tell you how much you owed, down to the penny. With my mom, there is no such thing as rounding; she pays to the exact penny and demands payment to the penny. She always wants to be the best and sets her goals accordingly. This trait drove her to work constantly and to gain the respect and adulation of her employers. All told, it brought her professional success.

It also meant that she was never around. And when she was, it was to work on extra projects from her work. My sister and I would help her, doing the handwork of physically folding mail, stuffing envelopes, and stamping. At one point in my life, I could stamp 1,000 envelopes in about fifteen minutes and collate/stuff 500 envelopes in about an hour and a half. But my mom was always faster. Mom told me once she was paid less than $3 per hour when she first started in the business. It's no wonder I grew up with only my sister.

My sister and I were on the reduced lunch program at school, and even back then, I tried to help save money by skipping meals. For every meal I didn't eat, we saved seventy-five cents. Those added up, and I'd use the money to buy things for around the house, bringing them home and putting them away before anyone could see.

The concept of capitalizing on the system to save wasn't foreign to me. When we first arrived in the US, my parents had food stamps. My dad, like many Vietnamese men, smoked. You can't buy cigarettes or alcohol with food stamps, but that didn't mean people with food stamps didn't want cigarettes or alcohol. My parents discovered a clever trick: because they had cash from their day jobs and cash was in short supply for many other people, they'd buy food stamps at a lower price. For example, they may buy $100 worth of food stamps for $80. Because they were legitimately using the stamps for food, it was a win-win and a smart way to augment income.

We also bought most everything in bulk and used coupons prolifically. My parents' small house was like a warehouse at times. We loaded up on whatever was on sale. Luckily, we had many people who shared the cost—and the food.

STUNTED SOCIAL GROWTH

At Luther Jackson, I kept my self-esteem high and excelled academically, winning awards and breezing through the advanced classes.

Luther Jackson was also the first time I began to sense the socioeconomic gap that distanced me from my classmates. I noticed many of the boys hit growth spurts. They began to lift weights and grow. I, for the most part, did not.

I also noticed people were dressing up more and paying more attention to their appearance. Girls became interesting to me, in a different way than they were before. There were social events, like Sadie Hawkins dances and theater productions. There were sports teams and clubs.

Financially, I wasn't able to participate in any events that happened outside of school hours. My parents worked all the time—and there would have been no way they could have picked me up. I rode the bus. If I didn't get on it to ride home, I'd be facing a three-hour walk.

I am not mad or regretful about missing out on the social aspects of middle school. It was a simple matter of looking at the facts: my situation did not allow for it. It is also a fact that when many kids my age were growing and honing their social networks, I was not privy to those bonding experiences.

Don't get me wrong, I still had friends—one beautiful girl who came from a very poor family and excelled academically; a "nerdy" boy who didn't quite make it into the gifted program; and another quiet girl whose height and size left her feeling distant. We all hung out, joked, and ate lunches together. We were a group of outcasts that found comfort in each other.

ACCIDENTAL HEARTBREAK

Just because I was a little socially stagnated didn't mean I didn't have chances with girls.

Well, sort of.

We had multiple families live with us in our little home. In our community, when one family became successful enough to get a place of their own, another family would move in. I developed a good relationship with these families—especially those who had kids around the same age as mine. But like I said, I was not interested in Vietnamese girls...well, that's not entirely true.

The father who built our basement had a daughter with a strong network of friends and family in the area. One of her visitors, a young lady I developed a crush on, would come over frequently with her family. Once or twice, we even had group sleepovers, innocent stuff. We'd play hide-and-seek and games like Monopoly. (I'm really good at Monopoly.)

The girl and I spent a lot of time together, and I thought she was cute. But at that age, we didn't know what girlfriend and boyfriend meant, and we never talked about it. It was purely friendship: our families became close, and I even played badminton with her dad.

One day, I got a call from one of my supposed friends. We were chitchatting, having an awkward conversation, probably, because I'm not great at talking on the phone. Suddenly, my friend asked me a question I wasn't prepared for.

"So, what do you think of that girl?" he asked.

"She's pretty cool and nice," I said.

"Oooohhh, you must really like her, huh? You want to be girlfriend/boyfriend?" he said in a tone that made me think he was joking around, teasing me. Though I *did* like her, I thought this was just a call between guys, so I denied it. The more he pressed, the more I denied, even making up reasons why I didn't like her just to get him off my case.

"OK, so you're sure? You're sure?" he asked, one last time.

"Yeah, there's nothing there. I don't like her, OK?"

The next time the family came over, I ran over to play badminton with them, like I always did. But the girl wouldn't come out of the van. Her sister told me it was because she'd been crying a lot. It turned out my "friend" had her on the line the whole time, along with a group of her female friends. So not only was she humiliated, but all her friends heard it too.

I never saw her again. Even though they continued to come over, she never would get out of the van. I couldn't even get her number to call her.

Then and now, I feel terrible. To this day, I still think about it—about why I acted so out of character and lied to impress my "friend" on the phone, and about how I hurt someone I cared about.

If I haven't gotten over it yet, there's a good chance this sixth-grade heartbreak story will go down with me.

BACK TO BASICS

Life at Graham Road Elementary School felt so much easier than my time at Luther Jackson. As rough as Kingsley Commons was, I enjoyed living there. There were many immigrant and low-income families there. There always seemed to be kids playing something in the grassy middle area—soccer, hide-and-seek. It was not uncommon to see thirty or more kids trying to play soccer with one ball in that field, or even in the street. My sister and I were two of them.

Unlike it would be just a few years later, my social life at

Kingsley Commons was amazing. I was one of the kids that was better at playing any sport. Because Graham Road was located right by our townhouse, I was able to participate in clubs and stay after school. I not only felt included in the social network there but I also felt like a valued part of it.

Academically, too, I continued my stride. I was always an entire grade ahead in math, and I had good relationships with all my teachers. My fourth-grade teacher gave points for extra credit academic work, and those points accumulated as time. We earned minutes we could take off during the school year. I played the system well, and by halfway through fourth grade, I'd accumulated so many points that I could have taken the rest of the year off. I didn't, of course. Instead, I took every afternoon off and went to play basketball—or whatever sport was on the agenda—with our popular and well-loved gym teacher.

After school most days, I'd play with a big, awkward kid with glasses whose face would turn completely red when he blushed at the smallest things. We were completely different physically, socially, and academically—but no one was closer to me back then. We saw the humanity in one another, regardless of it all.

When we moved into the house, even though I was farther away from my friend, he visited often. After school, he'd walk to our house, and we'd play in the backyard, climbing trees and making paths. The Vietnamese woman who rented a room at the time couldn't understand my friend, and he couldn't understand her. But they always laughed together. I think he was escaping from his home life too, in a way. He was my best friend.

CULTURE CONNECTION?

The Vietnamese community in Northern Virginia is rather large, and it was important to my parents—particularly my mother—that I stay connected to my heritage. To facilitate that, and because it would keep us busy, they insisted my sister and I take Vietnamese classes during the summer months.

I thought I was the high achiever in the class. I excelled at the different subjects within the classroom and outside of the classroom. But, when it came time for the awards ceremony at the end of summer, I was shocked when my name wasn't called.

I *was* Vietnamese. And I *was* the best student.

I was pissed that the son of the teacher won multiple awards, so I wrote off the course. I decided I was never going back because the whole thing felt unfair after that. My parents tried to get me to return, but I flatly refused. In retrospect, they likely wanted me to take the Vietnamese classes because their English was, and is, very shaky. It was for the sake of not just my learning but also for our ability to communicate. After I refused to take the classes, we strictly spoke Vietnamese at home, on purpose. I spoke English everywhere but in my own house.

My mom, in particular, tried hard to keep me connected to my culture because she is exceedingly protective. She has always been afraid to lose me—either physically or mentally—over time.

Both of my parents believe in fortune-telling, a sort of Vietnamese version of the horoscope. When they were looking into my future when I was a baby, they saw my fate: I would drown. So, they never let me swim. Little did they know that when we first came over to the US and stayed at my uncle doctor's house, I spent a lot of time at the bottom of his indoor pool. They were also very cautious of me going out in general, but that was rooted in a more socioeconomic fear. They didn't want me to get in some kind of trouble they'd have to pay to get me out of.

My mom held both my sister and I tightly, I believe, because she and my dad didn't get along well. We were all she had, her reasons for throwing everything else away.

My mom has an incredible intellect and memory, especially when it comes to numbers. Back in Vietnam, she'd put it to use, helping her parents build a textile empire—one that grew to be, essentially, the Nike of Vietnam. She was a walking ledger, able to do real-time accounting. This proved especially helpful in her ability to sell. Having grown up in affluence, one of her hobbies as a young woman was buying and appreciating diamonds. To this day, she can scrutinize and rate every diamond, down to the smallest detail.

Needless to say, my mom grew up exceptionally wealthy, eating in all the best restaurants and living in one of her parents' four houses, one of which was within walking distance of the palace in Saigon. She doesn't talk much about what transpired during her formative years, but you can tell she's developed a taste for the finer things in life. This taste is almost literal: she also has the ability to smell a dish and season it appropriately.

My maternal grandfather was known for being complicated, unyielding, and religious about the temperature of his food. If his soup wasn't warm enough, he'd refuse to eat it and send it back—a stereotypical aristocrat, or so we thought. Once, when I was a baby, I reached up and took off his glasses. Apparently, that was big deal, because everyone still talks about it. They couldn't fathom that he let someone get so close to his face, believing it to be a sign that he must have loved me.

FINDING MY LIMITS

Like everyone, I've had moments in my life that showed me what my limits are. An early one for me was way back in fourth grade. I always played football with the guys after school—but this wasn't two-hand touch. We tackled. We kept score. We wanted to win.

One game got particularly interesting. I caught the ball and started running toward the end zone. I got stood up—tackled but not taken down yet—by a couple guys from the other team. Then, another of their players came in, piled on, and threw me to the ground.

No big deal, right? That's football.

As the pile started to loosen, there was jawing going on amongst the guys.

Again, no big deal. That's football!

As I was walking away, a player from the other team smacked me in the back of the head—and then it was on.

In the Eastern culture I was raised in, the head is especially symbolic. You bow with it. Do you tolerate someone hitting you in the head out of the blue? Hell no. I was young, but I knew that much.

I snapped, turning around and going after the other team. I don't think I even remember which kid hit me in particular, but it didn't matter. Then, my team came to defend me, and it grew. I don't throw punches and didn't then either; I'm more of a "get you to the ground" guy—but still, it was a brawl.

I don't recall anything coming of the fight injury-wise, but I do recall understanding in that moment that while I am good-natured and I believe in the good in people, I have limits.

Don't worry: as an adult, I'm not walking around worried about someone smacking me in the back of the head. I have bigger things to worry about, like whether Starbucks will spell my name right on my venti mocha frap.

That threat is gone, but my limits are still there. Although I am giving of my time and space, I am also highly aware of people I let into my life. If someone has purposely done me wrong or I feel as though they have bad intentions, I don't let those people in, especially when it comes to my family or my finances.

This approach has helped me in the business world because I have my radar up all the time, especially when I'm presented with situations where I feel like my integrity may be violated or if people are taking advantage of me.

PRETENSION AND HYPOCRISY: TWO RED FLAGS

My radar is especially up when it comes to pretension and hypocrisy, both of which I cannot stand—and for good reason.

When I broke the girl's heart in sixth grade, I was being hypocritical and pretentious. I was the bad guy. I was worried about what some guy I barely kept in contact with thought more than being true to myself, and I hurt a girl I cared about in the process. I can't stand what I did, and it affects me more than I let on. That's why I look out for these qualities in others, because I know how ugly they can be.

PRETENSION

I cannot stand pretense. Why have a Gucci handbag when you can't afford it? When you have little, why try to act like you have more? When you're not knowledgeable about a topic, why pretend to be an expert? To me, it is far better to look at things objectively: either you have something, or you don't. No pretending necessary.

This concept is difficult, though, because it's so deeply ingrained in so many of us. My dad, like my best friend, grew up with less and felt he needed to tell bigger stories to be heard. Whenever my dad got backed into a corner or felt like he was on the losing end of an argument, for example, he'd revert to using my sister and I as leverage by saying some version of, "Well, look at my kids. They're better." I grew tired of people telling grandiose stories and trying to outdo each other. Don't get me wrong: I love Monday morning quarterbacking and joking around as much as the next guy. And while stories and jokes are generally harmless and some of my best friends' stories are pretty darn funny, it's when those stories become a part of someone's character and manifest into actions that it becomes problematic. Luckily, neither my dad nor my friend needed to buy expensive objects or bet our family's future on pretense. Suffice it to say that I got a bad taste in my mouth for pretension early from seeing people behave in this way, and as I've continued to see it in others since. When I see it, in a business setting or a casual setting, I question the person's integrity—and once that's gone, you can't get it back, in my book.

We are all pretentious at times. We're all human. As with being pretentious, the impact, for me, boils down to intention. There's a difference between using a story to protect yourself and using a story to put others down. There's a difference in using your power, your wealth, or your influence to manipulate rather than using it to help or make others comfortable.

HYPOCRISY

We all have slips of hypocrisy, but we should consciously

avoid it as much as possible. And, again, my radar is always tuned to search for it. I see this in engineering and in life. I've been in meetings where I know someone wants to win an argument or end a conversation, so they take a side they truly don't understand or believe. Then, they'll take the opposite action when they leave the room—or even months later. Or an idea or solution to a problem is presented, and they'll say it's wrong—only to do it down the road anyway. That's poor character, and I don't work with people with poor character. I can't trust them.

Of course, I believe people can change their minds, and that's not hypocrisy. But changing their convictions?

Life is filled with people who act as if they're morally righteous. But in the end, you often find out that they themselves cannot live up to the standards they set. For example, is it morally wrong to steal? Is it morally wrong to steal a loaf of bread when your wife and kids are starving? Is it morally wrong to buy something on Amazon through your work computer? All can be considered some form of stealing, yet certain scenarios are more socially accepted.

We are all hypocritical at times because we're all human. As with being pretentious, the impact, for me, boils down to intention: it's when a person does what they go out of their way to preach against that's unnerving.

PROJECTIONS

At the end of the day, those who are pretentious or hypocritical are hiding their own respective insecurities. And while it may be OK to have insecurities, it is *not* fine to project those insecurities on others.

Consider, for example, the elitism around someone scoffing at an opinion just because the statement-giver doesn't have a PhD. Or a person who dresses nicely purely to make others feel less-than. These actions are not reflections of the other parties involved. They're projections from the internal insecurities of the scoffer and the overdresser.

As for me, I try not to judge or impart my beliefs on others. If people want to be a part of my life and take on some of what I say and do, great. If they have a better way contrary to what I say or do, great. It's only if your actions start to affect my life...then we'd need to have a talk. I don't condone projecting and am comfortable knowing that I can only live my life to the best of my abilities.

MY ACHILLES' HEEL (ISN'T MY HEEL)

Once, in the grassy area outside our Kingsley Commons townhome, I was brought to my knees.

Not by any revelation, but by a bat to the gut.

My friends and I were playing a makeshift rotating baseball game. It was my turn to be the catcher, and the batter in that case had a strong follow-through. I caught it with my stomach.

I fell to the ground in tears, the wind more than knocked out of me. I thought back to a common scene from some of my favorite Chinese martial arts movies dubbed in Vietnamese—my only pastime besides playing outside—where the hero tries to create chi, or power. Part of how the heroes in the films create their chi is to sit in the Buddha position, focus on their breath, and meditate.

Growing up in Eastern culture, regulating the chi was a big deal. It was an especially big deal to a little kid who watched *Legend of the Condor Hero* repeatedly and had just gotten whacked in the stomach with a baseball bat.

So, I did it. I remembered my movies, sat in the Buddha position, and did breathing exercises. Good or bad, it did help me go from being hysterical to semi-calm. Although calm, I was still in excruciating pain every time I took a breath, and I had a massive bruise. I never told my parents, though, because it wouldn't have mattered. We didn't have insurance. I went through weeks of pain, sure I'd broken my ribs, until it either dissipated or I just got used to it.

To this day, if someone even gently hits me the wrong way

in that certain part of my stomach, I will fall to the floor wheezing. I think part of a loose rib bone is poking at my lung. But take that for what it's worth; I already told you I'm not a doctor.

This was a challenge when I began doing hardcore martial arts later in life because it didn't matter who hit me there or how hard. I'd go down every time, my breath gone.

Before the bat incident, I had fallen off the monkey bars and broken my right forearm. We didn't have the money for a doctor, so my parents wrapped my arm in some leaves they bought at the Vietnamese store that they must have believed would heal it. It healed on its own, as broken bones do over time. But it took weeks, if not months, and was extremely painful.

Through all of this, though I've revealed that I'm probably a little broken, there's one common denominator: that remaining calm matters. I take care to teach my kids this as often as possible.

Keeping calm is what helped me on that grassy patch. It's what helped me when my arm was wrapped with smelly leaves. It's what helped me when I was booking comedians with crazy-detailed riders as a member of SAB at Rose. It's what has helped me a million times since, in any situation that is chaotic. I don't automatically sink into the Buddha position like I did back then, but the point is the same.

PLANTING NEW ROOTS IN THE US

When we arrived in the United States after a long journey, we moved in with my mom's younger brother, a well-known doctor in Northern Virginia. Though he helped us with food and shelter—and even gave us a Pinto—it was a tenuous time for everyone involved. As with any new circumstances, conflicts arose on many different levels.

My parents knew we needed to move out of that house as soon as possible, so they scrambled to find new jobs in a new country. At the time, my dad was trying to get his draftsman degree in the States, but he couldn't see the drawings anymore. It was a blow to him and to our future.

As soon as we could, we moved to our own place in Kingsley Commons. By the time we got there and I started at Graham Road, I had already learned English from watching television, especially *Three's Company*. It helped that I'd had some English tutoring in the refugee camp before we immigrated, so I caught on quickly. I was one of the fastest people to graduate ESL Graham Road had ever seen.

It was the start of another chapter. Luckily, I already had

gotten my souvenir in the US in the form of a sliding door, my curious head poking through, and lasting stitches.

RUMINATIONS AND ILLUMINATIONS

In business or technology, I pride myself on being a fundamentalist, breaking everything down to their foundational elements. That's likely why I've been a little more successful than other people who are likely far smarter than me: extreme compartmentalization in times of extreme complexity.

For example, there's a tendency for young engineers (I was one of them) to overdesign in order to show that they know all the different theorems, essentially complicating things for the sake of complicating things. In my view, if you want to challenge yourself, the most successful—and most difficult—way to approach a problem is to see what you can do to solve it with the fewest parts.

In work and in life, I go with the simplest way to get things done. That means a lower chance of failure and fewer variables that could impact or halt progress. Staying calm helps in that simplification because it means you can avoid the minutia of distractions.

Because of this side of me, my wife often tells me she never wins an argument. To me, the small pieces of arguments *are* the minutia. What is the core problem at hand? What are we really talking about?

When my wife says that, I tell her that she certainly has won arguments with me. Lots of them.

"The reason you don't remember is that when I see I'm wrong, I admit it and move on. If I know I'm going to lose, there's not a good reason to continue. So the argument becomes a nonargument."

It doesn't bother me to be wrong. In actuality, I love the challenge of being wrong. If there is no chance of being wrong, what's the point of working on the problem in the first place? There must be that excitement of pushing our own limits. For me, being complacent or working on a problem that I've already mastered is excruciating.

Unfortunately, the hardest challenges in life are the ones that are situational or as a result of a complex web of decisions (even ones that were not our own). For example, I did not choose to be born into the circumstances and situations that formed my upbringing. Fate? In Eastern cultures, how you lived your past life influences your current fate. How cruel must I have been in my former life? During much of my youth, I blamed the world for what I didn't have. I hated the inequality, hated being hungry, hated being in physical and emotional pain all the time. There were a lot of times I wondered whether I could continue.

It wasn't always easy, I admit. But I found a way.

chapter *five*

SURVIVAL

Vietnam, 1979. *We float more. There is one barrel of fresh water for us all, but it is guarded by a guy with a gun. Dad is able to find a hose somehow and siphon some fresh water for us in the dark of night. A father and son start to reuse their own water. It makes everything smell. I bet my sister can smell it too. It would be impossible not to. I don't know how much longer we'll be floating.*

* * *

Our first attempt at leaving Vietnam left us stranded at sea. But we survived—which you know, because you've read this far.

Our second boat ride, in late 1980, was, according to my mom, free—to make up for the first failed attempt. What a deal.

My mom's younger sister, traumatized by the events of the first trip, chose not to make a second attempt—as did all my mom's other cousins, except for my six-fingered uncle.

This trip was successful, but not without incident. We were pirated at one point, and there was a struggle. I was young, so my memory comes in spurts. I know I was wearing a collared shirt, and somehow it came off and fell in the water. It made a heavy sound when it hit, a *bloop*, then sank. That seemed odd at the time. Why didn't it stay afloat like the clothes of the others?

I asked my mom about the memory years later: it turns out that my grandmother—who, having owned a textile business, was a phenomenal seamstress—had sewn gold into the collar of the shirt. Though she and my grandfather had lost much of their wealth after Black April, they managed to creatively hide some of it.

I had no idea. I was a little kid, and a shirt was a shirt. (I still kind of feel that way today, and I'm not a little kid. OK, maybe a big kid.)

My family tells me we were pirated other times on that trip, too, and I'm sure they're right. But I only remember the one, and the *bloop*.

When we landed in Thailand, we barely had anything left.

I was shirtless, wearing only a pair of pajama pants. The villagers approached our fishing boat, trying to take what little we had. Adults went after the adults, and a group of kids surrounded me. Some were kicking and hitting me, and others were trying to pull off my pants. I distinctly recall holding onto my pajama pants for dear life, struggling there on the beach. It was then that the captain of our boat, a large man (in Vietnamese perspective) came and put me on his shoulders.

After that, the Thai police came. We were too early for the whole refugee camp process, so they didn't have any place for us to stay. We slept outside the station under police cars at night. Everyone on our boat was there, laying under one car or another. It was cold on clear nights, especially because we didn't have possessions to cover ourselves with.

We were homeless for three days. Then, we went to our first of many refugee camps.

BREAKING MY HEAD...EVERYWHERE

I have cracked my head open in every country I've ever been to, starting with the first one: Vietnam.

I always joke that I could never afford a souvenir.

My grandparents had a spiral staircase, and I personally

think my sister pushed me while I was walking down it. She would tell you that story a different way. The rest isn't disputed, though. My dad was wearing a white collared shirt, as many Vietnamese men do. He picked me up and drove me on his scooter to the hospital. By the time we'd arrived, the shirt was soaked red.

In Thailand, at one of the refugee camps, a teenager threw a pail across a bathhouse and cracked me in the head. It was the same thing—blood, stitches, all that. I was fine, but the boy who threw the pail suffered severe punishment from his family. They made him kneel for several days in the crowded facility, not allowing him anything besides rice and fish sauce. It got so bad that I went to them and begged that they stop the punishment. It had been an accident, after all. Even as a young child, I was slightly different than many. Saving face for your family is big deal in Asian cultures, but I just wanted the boy to be able to get up.

I met him again, years later. He came with a group in the nineties to visit others from our boat who lived in Virginia. At that point, he was in his twenties and a big guy. We reminisced about the punishment, and he laughed, though I'm sure it was traumatic for him too.

Even a stopover at Singapore for only several days before taking a flight to the US provided the perfect opportunity for me to get more stitches on my head. My sister and I were playing tag—and, as you can guess, I fell, hit my head on a rock, and received stitches.

I can't remember all of what happened in Galang, but I am sure I spilled blood from my head somehow. Even the US did not spare me of a souvenir. A sliding door at Sleepy Hollow Elementary gave me my last scar. Turns out, that happens when you stick your head through it as someone is pulling it closed.

When I look in the mirror today, most of the six scars are difficult to notice. The memories of how I got them are slowly fading. I am sure my friends who read this will make comments like, "That explains a lot." Stubborn, resolute, and hardheaded are proper descriptions for how I have become.

These scars, though, are more than joke-starters. They're constant reminders of how unfortunate—and fortunate—my life has been. While no one wants to get stitches in refugee camps lacking sanitation in third-world countries, I did survive. And I turned out relatively normal—at least, I think.

GALANG II

The police sent us to a refugee camp eventually—and then two more after that. We were in Thailand for several months, moving from place to place. Then, we were moved off to what would become our home for the next year: Galang II Refugee Camp in Indonesia.

We tried to make Galang II feel like home. It was essentially island living—grass, blanket mattresses. When we first arrived, we helped build some of the homes we would come to live in. The passengers from our boat stayed somewhat together. I remember that my dad hung out with the men, and sometimes the group would try to hunt for food. My mom spent time with the women, cooking and gardening.

Another detail I remember about Galang II specifically is the Spam provided by the US government. We ate a lot of it. I also recall the rice, a bag of which they distributed to each family. Sometimes, we'd take the bag of rice and trade it for fish or other items we could get from the locals.

No matter how good we were at bartering, finding poultry or beef was always very difficult. At one point, and I don't remember how, we got ahold of a chicken to share among the entire village. My sister and I, being the littlest ones there, got one of the drumsticks. We sucked absolutely everything out of that drumstick. The bone was white, marrow sucked—absolutely nothing left.

To this day, when I eat chicken, I eat it to the bone. Only now, I prefer Bill Miller's fried chicken. Of all the places I could go to, why Miller's? Sure, there's great iced tea, but the main reason is that it's reasonably priced. It was one of the first places I frequented when I got out of college, so the taste has grown on me.

Besides the chicken, another favorite memory from Galang II is when we found the perfect stream for bathing on the island. Not only that, but something about the water helped us get rid of the horrible lice problem most of our community had developed hopping from camp to camp. Extra refreshing.

THE SADDEST PARTY

That holiday season, the adults in the camp wanted to throw a party to celebrate the holiday. Plans were made: they'd cut up fruits and vegetables they'd picked for the punch. The big problem was alcohol. It was very hard to find.

One man was able to barter with the locals to secure some alcohol, and the date of the party arrived. The adults mixed the alcohol to make the punch in a giant bowl for everyone to share. They had a hearty, fun time.

I heard my first scream of the night around what had to be midnight. Here, my memories go in and out.

Next, I remember my dad falling very ill. My uncle—who did not drink that night—carried him to the road to hitch a ride to Galang I, where he could be treated.

When we arrived at the makeshift barracks hospital, the doctor called my mom, my sister, and I into the room. I saw five men lined up on cots, each with toe tags. Their skin was black—not even their skin, but under their skin tissue. It is hard to describe, though I can still see it clearly.

My dad was the fifth of the toe-tagged men. The four others died.

It turned out what they had bartered for and assumed was alcohol was methanol, which destroyed their livers and sent their bodies into shock.

To this day, my uncle jokes that rats saved my dad, as both he and my sister were born in the Year of the Rat.

ONE IN THREE

We had a Vietnamese teacher at Galang II, one who did not come with us on the boat. He had a cute daughter about my sister's age. The three of us played together often. I learned my first English words from her dad.

After we'd been at Galang II for about a year, coincidently, we got notice that they were leaving. Others from our boat made refuge in the US and other countries earlier. However, we were delayed because my mom had tuberculosis.

After she recovered, the US accepted us, and we were also ready to leave.

The girl, my sister, and I had been on the island the longest. We were experienced of our surroundings. One day, we set out to play hide-and-seek, as we often did. I was a little guy and pretty clever, so hiding was my specialty. After a while, though, I realized nobody was coming to look for me, so I left my hiding place and tried to find the girls. I finally found my sister, who was also hiding, but we could not find our friend.

After searching for a long while, we walked back to her house, hoping she was there.

It turns out she'd gone home because she'd started to feel ill.

"It's probably nothing," her dad said. "She's come down with a fever and is feeling pretty bad. Don't worry about it. Everything will be fine."

When my family and I stood waiting for our transportation to the boat the next day, I looked around to see who was there. She was supposed to be coming with us, but neither her nor her father were around.

My parents told me she still wasn't feeling well, so she couldn't leave. That made sense to me at the time. We hadn't been able to leave earlier because my mom had TB, so I understood. I thought she must have the flu or something similar.

Sometime later, after we'd arrived in the US, word made it to us that this little girl and her father were also in the US—and in Maryland, which was close to us. We went to visit and found out she had been admitted to Johns Hopkins Hospital. That was the reason they'd finally been able to come to the US—because the hospital wanted to study her.

She had been attacked by some sort of brain-eating parasite.

When we walked into her hospital room, she was nonresponsive. She didn't know anything or anyone. The nurses had to bathe her and get her in and out of bed, and she didn't have control of any of her functions.

Her dad was a mess as he spoke to us, indicating he'd also lost his wife on the trip over to the US.

To this day, part of my anger toward Vietnam or my ambivalence to the Vietnamese side of me is that her family was subjected to such horror. That the random chance it happened wasn't entirely random: it was the result of all us having to run away from a country that didn't want us.

People see me, and they see that I try to do good for the

world. Some think it's an excuse or a show. I can tell you unequivocally that it is not. That could have easily been me, or it could have been my sister. We were literally in the exact same area at the exact same time. Though I don't tell her story much because it is heartbreaking, I am intrinsically motivated by her, and I know the probability for death is one in three.

YIN/YANG

One of my favorite movies is *Up* (That's what happens when you have kids. Let it go. Let it go.), the animated film about a man who got left behind when society advanced too quickly around him, and he lost people he loved in the process. He ended up alone in an old house. That character and I share a bit of the same plight: he's a guy who lived his life, paid his dues, but yet at the end of the day, there was nothing left. That movie makes me perspire around the eyes, I admit, because it speaks to those feelings of abandonment.

Good Will Hunting also gets me, in which Matt Damon's character has the "me against the world" attitude. I have that in me too: a guy without a country, without a heritage, not really Vietnamese but not really American. While I find comfort and can relate to both worlds, neither world encompasses who I am. That certainly further steeled me to the world.

All of these hardships and realizations made me who I am today. Sometimes those realizations hit harder than others.

I say I am a guy without a world, but I'm actually a guy with many worlds: investor groups, nonprofit groups, friends, a few really good friends, family. I am home here, now. But even in these familiar circumstances, I am uniquely alone.

When we arrived in the States, I was angry at our plight. I wanted to get out and be on my own as soon as possible, away from the abandonment. And in many ways, I did. In many ways, I am independent to a fault. That sense of belonging was lost during the voyage. That sense of emotional/social reliance was lost during my youth.

Today, if I'm around a group of Westerners, I behave in a certain way. In a group of Easterners, I behave in a different way. Having leveraged those two worlds to become successful, in many ways, I still feel slightly lost and yearn for a belonging I won't feel.

This is not something I can or would change. It's just a fact.

RUMINATIONS AND ILLUMINATIONS

My sister is and always has been my bridge to the Vietnamese community, and in some ways, to my parents. She's also my anchor.

When we first arrived in the US, my parents worked almost around the clock. My sister, three years older than me, raised me—cooking, cleaning, babysitting. When we needed to go to the market, we went together. We didn't have much parental supervision at home.

She also let me hang around with her and her friends. I beat her at all her girly games, like hopscotch and such. She would tell you she let me win to build up my self-confidence, but that is not how I remember it.

Yes, we always had another family or person living with us to offset costs, and those people were adults, six in total throughout my childhood. We learned something from each of them, and I think they learned from us too. But at the end of the day, they were all leaving at some point. It was me and my sister who were consistently there for one another, always.

Today, we joke together and talk often. She's a PharmD working for the FDA, so she's highly intelligent and successful in her own right. (She paid me to put that in here.) I know I can sometimes have an internal arrogance that comes from knowing who I am and being eternally introspective. If anybody could challenge that part of me, it would be my sister.

In my youth, I likely did not appreciate the fact that another person was dealt worse cards than me and still lived the American dream. She, being older, probably remembers more of the trauma, had more responsibilities, and still had to deal with an arrogant (rightly so) younger brother. However worse her cards, she still came out on top. In this game, I fold to her raise.

I can't write too many more nice things about her, though, because she'll get a big head.

chapter / *six*

WE END AT THE BEGINNING

Vietnam, 1979. *We finally hit land again—but not a sandy beach. There is mud. Thorns. Everyone is so happy. It is like a movie—people kissing the ground. We are so elated. So hungry. There are little crabs everywhere. Someone gets bitten on the toe, and I see blood in the water. I don't care. I reach down anyway, like the others, and grab the crabs. I start eating. The taste, the feeling is extraordinary. No food will taste that good again.*

* * *

When we finally hit land after being stranded at sea for seven days and seven nights, after I'd eaten the best crab of my life, we started to walk toward civilization. We had little to no possessions with us. Soon, we encountered a less-than-friendly militia: we were back in Vietnam, and they promptly arrested us.

My memories are spotty here, too, because of my age, but I specifically recall my parents drilling my sister, telling her to use a fake name. We all used fake names because the militia was interviewing everyone. My parents did not want our last name revealed because of our wealth. Whether that was for our protection or because my parents did not want anyone to find out we were associated with the "boat people," I don't know. But I do know they told my sister, over and over, to use her new last name when confronted by the soldiers who were walking around with guns.

"Your name is Quynh Tran, not Quynh Duong. Do you understand? Your first name is Quynh. Your last name is Tran."

They never interviewed me. In the end, they put us all in prison in the middle of nowhere, Vietnam. The prison was under tribal law, which meant, in short, that whatever they said was law. I was placed in the women's prison with my mom, and my sister was put in the men's prison with my dad.

We were in prison for two or three weeks before they released the women and children. Because my sister was in the men's side, my dad literally shoved her to the line of children walking out, saying, "I don't know her. She's a kid. Let her go." She got lucky.

My dad and three uncles would not be so lucky. They spent months there. One of my uncles had it the worst. He was sent to a different prison to the south, where he was caned and whipped. He's never spoken of the trauma, but there's also a reason he didn't join us on the second round.

That's not to say the prison my dad was in was easy, by any means. The floors weren't concrete. South Vietnam is like Florida: most of the land is at or below sea level. The cells were made of bound bamboo. They served only rice—something my dad historically, and ironically, could not eat. He always ate bread or noodles instead—a very non-Vietnamese thing for a Vietnamese man to do. He'd developed a phobia of rice very early in his childhood, having grown up surrounded by the cheap grain when his family immigrated to South Vietnam after the Great Vietnamese Famine. He's never told us the whole story, but the phobia is legitimate.

Rice was all they served in prison, so at first, my dad ate the burnt rice at the bottom of the pan because it resembled a different grain. They stopped giving him that option, though, so he had to not only face his phobia, but rely on it for life.

The only time he's eaten rice as an adult, ever, was during those months in prison. It was either that or starve.

ALL THE GOLD IN SAIGON

After my sister, mom, and I were released from prison, we made our way back to my grandparents' house (well, one of them). They'd lost their other homes to the Communist regime, but their home in Saigon was the one they were allowed to keep.

I did not realize until much later in my life exactly how much my grandparents lost after the war, but my mom told me it was a tremendous amount of wealth. At that time in Saigon, they were still in the process of losing it. They gave my mom a bit of starting money so she could start a business while my sister and I stayed with them.

Business in Vietnam is not like business in the US. My mom would buy fabric at a distribution center, walk to the market, put a bamboo sheet down, and sell it in the streets. She sold in front of storefronts and was threatened multiple times, even at knifepoint. She kept moving throughout the streets of different towns in Vietnam, trying to make money.

When she had enough, she'd go buy my dad and my uncles cigarettes. Like in *Shawshank Redemption*, you can buy almost anything with a pack of smokes in prison. That holds true in Vietnam too. To deliver them, she had to travel a long distance, sometimes knocking on the doors of strangers and asking if she could spend the night, sometimes spending the night in the street.

Though she was using only the bamboo sheet as a store, my mom was a good businessperson. She became successful and made connections. At one point, a Chinese woman offered a storefront for her as long as they shared the profit. The currency for that profit, by the way, was bars of gold. To this day, she still talks about them.

It took a lot of bars of gold to get my dad and my uncles out of prison.

While my mom was working to get them out of the Communist prisons, we lived with our grandparents. They loved us, in many ways. Even my stern grandfather, the one who let me touch his glasses, softened a bit to us then.

STAY OR GO?

My grandparents not only knew about our attempt at leaving but they'd also helped pay for it. In Vietnam, everyone knows everyone, and our boat trip was sponsored by someone who lived in their town of origin, from the north.

They did not join us because they still had some wealth and probably would not have survived the voyage. They'd dispersed it and hid it, but some remained. Even though the Communist soldiers spent months literally living in one of the homes that they'd eventually seize anyway (just to see what they were hiding). And, to be frank, they were already old, even then. And their life was there.

That's just how war works. This technique wasn't communism-specific. If you truly want to take over an area, you get rid of the wealthy and educated people first. The same thing happened in Nazi Germany with the Jews. After the critical thinkers are gone or silenced, you can sway the minds of the rest with propaganda. It's a sad truth.

I remember my sister coming home with word problems like, "If one grenade will kill eight Americans, how many would three grenades kill?" My parents wanted to leave because they didn't want a future like that for me and my sister. When the Communists came, we needed to go. For whatever faults they may have, I am forever grateful to my parents for making that decision.

Later in life, my grandparents *did* sell everything and immigrate to the US. The whole time they lived stateside, they were scared that at any moment, they could be sent back. Truthfully, I don't know if it was good for them to come to the US. I'd visited my grandparents for the first time in Vietnam post-boat trip when I flew back in 1994. Even though they were obviously older, my grandfather would walk everywhere. He was faster than me. They had their regular spots—for coffee, for pho. But there was fear there too. Before night came, they'd lock up the house completely, including the sliding fence in front of the doors. That was their daily life for decades.

They ultimately left Vietnam to find freedom in the US, but in reality, what they found here was solitude. They lost their life, and they were confined to my uncle's house, not so free after all. That begs the question, of them and us all: how many of us are truly free?

RUMINATIONS AND ILLUMINATIONS

I've had a lot of choice in my life, and I'm lucky in that respect. I've made many big decisions, some good and some bad. Many of us have fought to get to a point where we had access to freedoms, but in order to use them, we have to ask critical questions of ourselves.

How many people who would call themselves independent thinkers are the same religion as their parents? How many live in or near the same town where they grew up? How can there be certain pieces of ourselves we don't question, and other pieces we feel are free?

How much freedom do we all truly have here, though? Are we steering or being steered?

Stereotypically, many Asians are pushed into fields like science, mathematics, or medicine. I pursued engineering but not because I had to. I chose it. My cousin is a successful wedding photographer in New York City, and she once said how lucky she felt not only to have found her passion in life, but to have it reflected in her work. She is never going to win a Nobel Prize, but that doesn't matter. The prize is her life and her happiness. That's the definition of a life well-steered.

That's what I want for my kids too. I want them to be able to look in the mirror at the end of the day and say, "I enjoy what I did today. It was fulfilling. It is not what I 'should' do, but it's what I have chosen. And I've done it to the best of my ability."

That is success, and I want my kids to have it. I want them to be motivated to do whatever they love and do it well. I want them to embrace and exercise their freedom, their chance to steer, because not everyone gets a chance to do that.

We've all heard the story about the farmer and the stockbroker. The farmer wakes up, works his tail off all day, and stops at dusk—only to do it all again the next day. It's a hard life, but one he wants. The stockbroker wakes up, goes to his stressful nine-to-five, and has dinner at a Michelin-star restaurant—only to do it all the next day because he is supposed to.

Of the two, who would be more likely to commit suicide? Who is truly happy?

Life is not about money or wealth, whether we're talking about investments or bars of gold. You do need a certain threshold, but after shelter, food, and the necessities, life should be about making yourself and those around you better. It's about doing what you love, having integrity, and making the world better as best you can. I am trying to do that more and more each day: trying to improve my life, trying to improve my family's life, and trying to improve the lives of those around me. I also have loftier goals of impacting the world in a positive way. I do not know whether my investments, my technological achievements, or my wife's charity will ultimately be impactful. I do know that it would be shame if we did not at least try.

While the hand I was dealt is objectively not desired—and while there have been times I've wondered whether I should have just closed my eyes—I am grateful to have made it this far in life.

Good, bad, or indifferent, I opened my eyes.

CONCLUSION

This is not the first immigration story, nor will it be the last. This is not the first story of growing up in poverty, of reusing paper towels two and three times, of feeling socially out of place—nor, again, will it be the last. Far from it.

At the end of the day, I went through a particular set of circumstances that shaped me. Of those circumstances, I have never once asked for pity or said, "Woe is me." That said, I acknowledge that the problems I faced were valid and formative, just as all big problems are.

This includes the ones you're facing now and will face later in your life. That's why I wrote this book. (Which, by the way—thanks for sticking around this long!)

Was life harder from my dad's perspective? Who grew

up poor but highly intelligent, got a glimpse of affluence when he married my mom, and lost both that autonomy and status at once? Was life harder from my mom's perspective, who had everything at one point yet had to turn to collating mail sixteen hours a day?

There are many truths here: when they brought me and my sister to the US, both my parents lost something. After they brought us to the US, me and my sister lost lots of things too. Had we all stayed in Vietnam, we collectively would have lost more.

The deck was never stacked in our favor, it seems. But everyone has their own demons, and we are not in competition with one another's scars. A problem is a problem, and a hardship is a hardship. Each of us experience these differently.

Though still vivid, the gravity of those difficult memories from my youth is starting to fade. The challenges I've faced at work and in my adult life, though they felt huge in those moments, don't feel that heavy anymore. Time does that. Perspective does that.

When you're in those challenging situations, though, your circumstances consume your mind. Though you may *intellectually* know people out there have bigger problems, you may struggle to conceptualize that fact because you're so focused on your struggles. How could you not be, right? Sometimes, doing so feels like an act of survival.

I know. I've been there.

Everyone—even a wealthy, intelligent person who seems to have everything—is going to run into a challenge from time to time that feels overwhelming. I don't want to offer boilerplate advice like "Time makes it better" or "Put one foot in front of the other and persevere,"—although, to be fair, both of those are true.

Instead, I'll offer you my experience: in my life, I've focused on self-reliance, independence, and inner strength. This faith in myself is not something you can find in a chapel or in a book. Its roots have grown strong out of necessity. It's evolved to the point that feeling failure has often motivated me or pressured me to do better.

In many of my dark moments, I've been able to turn to my ability to see pressure as fuel. Other times, in the darkest of the dark—the line between trust in myself and self-confidence has blurred, and my lack of the latter has felt particularly dimming. In those times, the pressure has been anything but motivating.

When it threatened to come crashing down—although I do have such an internal focus, which may not work for everyone—it was the opposite that kept me going. It was an *external* focus. Even at times when I didn't think people loved me, I still acknowledged that I didn't want bad things to happen to them. I didn't want them to be hurt by my actions.

We all have the capacity for both an internal and external focus. It's part of what makes us human. Though I'm certain no two ratios are the same, we all feel those pulls. Naturally, when you're in a hard spot, your understanding of the situation revolves around how it affects *you*. That makes sense—after all, you're seeing it through the lens of your own experience.

The perspective I hope to have offered here, through my story, is the kind that comes from the opposite approach. When we don't shut our eyes but instead shift our gaze to meet the moment—and to see the next.

ACKNOWLEDGMENTS

Thank you to my parents, **Nguyen Thi Hoa and Duong Van Khanh**. (Yes, the surname is first in Vietnamese culture.) While we may have had our differences, my world, *the* world, would not have been the same without you both. My accomplishments would not have been possible without your many sacrifices and contributions to my life. From making the tough decision to leave the comfort and relative affluence of Saigon to sacrificing your pride, working countless hours, preaching the right way to succeed, and doing whatever it took to survive, your impact on this world shall last.

Thank you to my sister, **Quynh-Van Tran** (Americanized and ironic, right?), who deserves the most thanks. We have been resilient. The odds were never in our favor, but we today live (in our respective ways) the American Dream. I cannot thank you enough for being there for me: through all the waves, through all the cockroaches, through all your bad cooking, through all the teasing (I can be cruel). Thank you, too, for reading through my various drafts and giving me advice along this book-writing process.

Thank you to my wife, **Janny Ly**. Your tenacity, generosity, and sense of community connected me back to a country that I had long forgotten. It is you who motivates me to help the Vietnamese community in Dallas/Austin. I was honored to provide resources to help you start Perspective Charity (perspectivecharity.org). And I continue to be amazed at your dedication to the betterment of children here and around the world. (Please visit Perspective's website if the cause inspires you. Volunteers and donations are celebrated.)

Thank you to my three children (**Anastasia, Athena, and Radiant**) for not disturbing me while I worked. (Wait, did that happen?) You are my inspiration for writing this book.

Thank you to **my close family, in-laws, cousins, and nephews** (no nieces, for some strange reason). While I may not mention it, I do respect what each of you have done and will continue to do to make your world—our world—better.

Thank you to **my distant family, uncles, aunts, and cousins**. The path toward making a life in America has been different for all of us. Each of us have our own unique set of stories and circumstances, each fraught with tears and laughter. I am glad that for the most part, our families remain in contact. I know I am never around, but hopefully we can change that in the future.

Thank you to **my family still back in Vietnam.** The worlds we live in are completely different, yet I am astonished how similar our day-to-day lives are.

Thank you to **the venture capitalists, vendors, customers, and professionals around the world who believe in me.** Thank you for enabling me to help the world. I want to specifically thank all of my business partners, especially my friend **Nick.** We've had a hell of a ride. You're a talent that the world needs, and I will continue to try to sway you from your pending retirement.

Thank you to **my groomsmen and groomswoman. CW, Ron, Chris, Diana, and William,** thank you for lifting the car off that pedestrian path. You have inspired me in countless ways. We've shared drinks, 10Ks, punches, late-night coffee poetry, and each other's lives.

Thank you to **my friends—my family—at Martial Way.** We had a lot of fun, didn't we? And the martial art was fun as well. I miss kicking your asses. Or was it the other way around? The memory is kind of blurry. Thanks for sharing your life and that moment in time with me.

Thank you to **my ASF friends** who later formed an engineering consulting firm, **Ascendant Engineering Solutions**. You guys are, by far, the best group of engineers I've ever worked with. Having worked at multiple companies and started multiple companies, the engineering talent at ASF and now AES is unmatched.

Thank you to **my college roommates** at Village Quarters. How we didn't get kicked out of that place, I don't know. Did we ever get our deposit back? **Game, Boog, Dog, Kork, Fix, Woman (an honorary roommate), Dan, Troy**, thanks for putting up with me, helping with SAB, and being a part of my college experience. All the bad parts of my personality are a result of living with you guys. I know…that's a badge of honor for most of you.

Thank you to **Rose-Hulman, the deans, and my professors**. I grew up a lot at Rose. A special thanks to **Dr. John Koshel**, who not only tutored/mentored me my senior year at Rose, but has helped me since.

Thank you to **all my friends**. I am poor at keeping in touch, but each of you have shaped me into the person I am today. Yeah, it is your fault!

Thank you to **Michelle Patterson** for introducing me to Scribe and **Suzi Sosa** for the personal introduction to **Tucker Max**. I want to thank **JT McCormick** for sharing his perspective on the process of writing a memoir. Thank you to **Jessica Burdg**, my Scribe writer. You have been nothing less than spectacular. Your professionalism, wit, humor, dedication, and sympathetic ear have gotten a callous heart to open. Jessica, it has been an adventure, and I very much thank you for the process and work. Do not be afraid to share your opinions and instincts. They are always welcomed and helpful.

ABOUT THE AUTHOR

DUNG DUONG is an entrepreneur, investor, and optic engineer who's dedicated to making our world a better place. Alongside his wife, Dung helps run Perspective Charity, a nonprofit working to give children the opportunity to become impactful doers, contributors, and leaders regardless of their economic or social situation. Dung wrote this book for his three children—Anastasia, Athena, and Radiant—in the hope that they find comfort, snicker at the infinitely bad jokes, and get a different perspective.